School Counseling

# THE PROFESSIONAL EDUCATION SERIES

Walter K. Beggs, *Editor*
Dean Emeritus
Teachers College
University of Nebraska

Royce H. Knapp, *Research Editor*
Regents Professor of Education
Teachers College
University of Nebraska

# School Counseling

## Theories and Concepts

*by*

### WILLIAM A. POPPEN

Associate Professor
Educational Psychology and Guidance
University of Tennessee, Knoxville

*and*

### CHARLES L. THOMPSON

Professor
Educational Psychology and Guidance
University of Tennessee, Knoxville

PROFESSIONAL EDUCATORS PUBLICATIONS, INC.
LINCOLN, NEBRASKA

*Dedicated to*
*Susan and Harriet*

Library of Congress Catalog Card No.: 73-86632

ISBN   0-88224-070-6

© Copyright 1974
by
Professional Educators Publications, Inc.

# Contents

# Preface

Since the early 1900s many people have expressed an interest in school counseling. Teachers, recognizing that they cannot have a positive impact on all of their students, have seen counseling as a means of helping young people to do better in school. Administrators, knowing that the schools are not capable of meeting all the needs of all the youngsters enrolled in them, have hoped that counseling would enable students to obtain increased benefits from admittedly imperfect educational programs. Parents, acknowledging that the influence they have on their children is limited, have called for counseling to help youngsters avoid some of the pains and pitfalls of growing up. Finally, social reformers have seen counseling in the schools as a means of decreasing maladaptive behavior, or of increasing proper behavior. For example, some have wanted to reduce the number of unwanted pregnancies among adolescents, and to decrease delinquency and other undesirable forms of conduct. Others advocate counseling that would increase the number of young people deciding to enter certain occupations. Still others, reformers who want to liberate children, have insisted that counseling ought to help youngsters to choose a life-style and to determine ways to live in accordance with their choices.

Expectations about what school-counselors should do have been varied and high. In fact, at one time or another counseling has been suggested as a treatment for almost every one of the "ills" of education. Even though special funds have been allocated, and special training programs established, the resources provided for counseling have not been sufficient. Counseling and guidance have had considerable positive effects upon schools and young people, but many tasks are yet unfulfilled. Today's students need even better counseling in order to deal with an increasingly complex occupational world and with rapid social change.

Interest in school counseling remains high because people know that counseling is sound in concept, and can be effective if carried out proficiently and systematically.

*School Counseling: Theories and Concepts* is an introduction to school counseling; it was written in response to the continued interest of teachers, parents, and citizens. The book begins by defining school counseling and reviewing its history and foundations. A number of theories basic to school-counseling practice are presented. Two chapters describe individual and group counseling in detail. Further on, some of the noncounseling functions of the school-counselor are summarized. Discussions of issues, trends, and research in school counseling are also presented. The book concludes with an annotated bibliography designed to provide guidance for further reading in the field of school counseling.

The authors wish to express their thanks to the following people for their assistance in the preparation of the manuscript: James D. McComas and Lawrence M. DeRidder for their support; Jean Cates, Susan Poppen, Harriet Thompson, and Naomi Thompson for their editorial assistance; and Lana Arms for typing the manuscript.

CHAPTER 1

# Foundations of School Counseling

## WHAT IS SCHOOL COUNSELING?

School counseling is one of the services offered by a school's guidance program. The other services include consultation (with parents and teachers) and coordination of school and community services, focusing on career education, student evaluation, placement, and follow-up.

We define school counseling as a *person-to-person relationship* in which one person helps another resolve an area of conflict that heretofore has not been resolved. The helper in the relationship, by virtue of his or her training and experience, is a counselor who attempts to assist the student in becoming an independent person capable of resolving his conflict situations (Thompson and Poppen 1972).

*Conflict,* in our definition, refers to any block that the student is experiencing in his development. Conflict areas include conflict with others, conflict with self (indecision), lack of information about self and the environment, and lack of the knowledge and skill requisite to personal goal achievement. While our definition, in the above statement, seems limited to one-to-one counseling, we do not mean to imply that group counseling is not an important function and an effective counseling method for counselors in elementary and secondary schools. Our basic definition of individual counseling would hold true for group counseling, which provides the counselor and the students with the advantage of greater opportunity for feedback on how their behavior affects other people. The group-counseling setting also offers more opportunities for practicing new behaviors before trying them in "outside" situations. Counseling, whether one-to-one or in groups, has the ultimate goal of behavior change

Various labels have been given to the persons receiving counseling. We choose to refer to the persons counseled by school-counselors as *students* because that is what children and adolescents are usually called. In 1958, when school counseling first received major federal support for the training and education of counselors, it was fashionable to refer to students receiving counseling as *counselees*. Counseling psychologists refer to persons receiving counseling as *clients*, and clinical psychologists and psychiatrists refer to members of their treatment population as *patients*. We view the counseling process as something beneficial for all students and not as reserved just for "sick" persons or for persons in deep trouble.

## Other Definitions of School Counseling

Is school counseling a remedial or a developmental process? Those who regard counseling as a remedial process would, of course, have the school-counselor working only with students who are in trouble. Such "trouble" would include behavior problems, failing in school, and potential dropping out and delinquency.

Those who regard school counseling as developmental see the counselor as focusing more on the population of normal students. Counseling, then, would stress the next step in the student's development and, as such, would not be reserved for problem students only. Developmental counseling would have a preventive rather than a remedial nature. "Counseling for all" would be the cry of the developmental school-counselor (Peters and Farwell 1967; Blocher 1966).

The counselor who can handle both the remedial and the developmental aspects of school counseling receives our vote of confidence. Rather than specializing entirely in students' problems or nonproblems, the school-counselor would do better to specialize in the individuality of each student.

## Is School Counseling Therapeutic Conversation?

Schofield (1964) made the point that psychotherapy (or counseling) was merely the purchase of friendship—that people are willing to pay for someone to listen to them. The breakdown of the family and the neighborhood-unit-living concept has apparently contributed to the lonely-person syndrome, or state of anomie, in our culture. School counseling offers the opportunity for active listening to what students are trying to communicate. Toffler (1970), in his book *Future Shock*, writes about the need for group-counseling-type experiences for individuals as they move from one transition point to another in their lives. Possibly culture shock can be diminished when people listen to one another.

## Is School Counseling a Decision-making Process?

Williamson (1950) has for several years stressed the importance of teaching decision-making skills in the counseling process. More recently, Gelatt, Varenhorst, and Carey (1972) have published some teaching units on decision-making for counselors to use with student groups. One primary focus of school counseling is to teach students how to become their own counselors so that they will be able to achieve independence by making their own decisions. School-counselors who keep their students dependent by making decisions for them would seemingly be missing the goal of helping students achieve autonomy through the mastery of decision-making skills.

## Is School Counseling a Problem-solving Process?

The school-counselor's role has a teaching focus. In addition to decision-making, the counselor is involved in teaching students the process of problem-solving. School counseling is based on the idea that all of us have problems and that some persons solve their life's problems while others are blocked. The counseling process is therefore directed toward the identification and practice of alternative problem-solving behaviors. Blocher (1966) describes the problem-solving counseling group as offering an experience where each student can counsel and be counseled. The problem-solving group is helpful to students who believe they are the only ones ever to suffer from a particular problem. Not only do they receive empathy from their fellow group members, but quite often they learn new approaches for the remediation of old problems and blocks.

## Is Counseling a Process of Self-Exploration and Self-Actualization?

Following Maslow's theory (1970) that higher levels of human needs cannot be achieved until lower-level needs are met, we conclude that school counseling is very much concerned with both the exploration and the actualization of the self. School counseling, by assisting students in removing blocks to meeting lower-level physiological and safety needs, opens the door for further personal development through the achievement of higher-level belongingness, love, self-esteem, and self-actualization needs. Exploration of self in the school-counseling process might involve looking at individual strengths and weaknesses through various diagnostic tests and inventories, or it could be done in a less-structured manner through a clinical-type interview or case-study procedure. Again, the group-counseling experience is useful in helping students identify and actualize their potential strengths. If we define self-actualization as becoming all that one can become in all areas of one's life, then we would want to include it as a school-counseling goal.

## Is School Counseling an Art or a Science?

The question of whether counseling is an art or a science was first posed by the Pepinskys in 1954. They viewed the counselor as a scientist-practitioner who acts first as a scientist, employing the methods of hypothetico-deductive thinking, and second as a practitioner. In this dual role, the counselor employs the scientific method of observation, inference, and assessment of behavior changes during and after counseling.

Effective school counseling does seem to be an art insofar as the development of the intangibles in the counseling relationship is concerned—for example, rapport, trust, acceptance, warmth, openness, and authenticity. However, significant progress has been made in the past five years in techniques of obtaining objective data for evaluating both the process and the outcome of counseling. In fact, the relatively intangible quality of empathy has been defined and classified according to levels and degrees by Carkhuff (1969).

With the advent of the age of accountability, school-counselors are finding it necessary to show how their counseling and noncounseling functions are making a positive difference in their students. Much of the counseling-outcome evaluation can be achieved through the identification of outcome-objectives, since these can be observed and, therefore, evaluated. For example, one such objective might read as follows: after completion of a series of counseling interviews (not exceeding ten in number), Joyce will be operating successfully on a grade-contract plan, which will earn her at least a passing grade in English. To be sure, such concrete objectives represent only the bare minimum of the outcomes of school counseling. Many of the higher levels of human need-fulfillment mentioned earlier cannot be measured by concrete, observable data. Even so, counselors can rely on data from self-reports and semantic-differential-type instruments to evaluate some of these intangibles of counseling-outcomes.

The school-counselor, then, finds himself conducting much of his work as a scientist. During the counseling interview, the counselor establishes hypotheses about the student's situation and evaluates the observed data to determine whether the hypotheses should be accepted or rejected in favor of a new set of hunches. The scientist role of the counselor also surfaces during the evaluation of his or her own counseling effectiveness.

## Is School Counseling a Profession?

According to Greenwood's definition (1962), an occupation attains professional status when both internal and external consensus are achieved on what services the occupation provides. Internal consensus refers to agreement among persons in the profession on what the role of the school-counselor should be. External consensus refers to agreement among persons outside the profession on what the school-counselor should do. Since the enactment of the National Defense Education Act of 1958, which provided for counselor training and other guidance services, considerable evidence has been gathered that indicates that we are reaching both internal and external consensus on the school-counselor's role.

## Level of Self-Disclosure Characteristic of Counseling Interview

In the early days of school counseling, counseling and other guidance services were sometimes a function of part-time teacher-counselors. Generally, a teacher with little or no training in counseling was released from teaching for a short time each day to do the counseling job. In such a part-time role, little time was available to develop the counseling relationship, even if the "counselor" had the necessary skill to do so. Therefore, much of the counseling consisted of little more than the giving of advice and information. The counselor was viewed primarily as a person who could provide information about getting into college or getting a job. With mainly vocational and educational problems being brought to the school-counselor, self-disclosure by students seldom went beyond the surface level. In the past decade, with better-trained counselors being hired in full-time counseling positions, evidence began to appear that students now trusted counselors enough to discuss their personal concerns with them. Thompson (1969) reported that among school-counselors' preferred and nonpreferred students, three problem categories (vocational, emotional, and educational) were discussed in counseling interviews. It was observed that more problems from the emotional-problem category appeared among the counselors' nonpreferred counseling group. Thompson's study would seem to support the notion that students are more comfortable in discussing emotional or personal concerns than the counselor is in listening to them. On the other hand, as Schofield (1964) pointed out, most professional therapists prefer to work with patients having fewer and less serious problems and, consequently, a higher expectancy for improvement.

It appears, therefore that the level of self-disclosure achieved in a counseling interview is a function of several factors: trust between the counselor and student; likability of the student; likability of the counselor; and the counselor's preference for the problem-type and problem-cause. From the observation of several counseling interviews, including our own, we have concluded that at least five levels of self-disclosure may appear. Lazarus (1969) developed a model based on five levels of self-disclosure, which he uses as a device for helping his patients examine the type of content they are disclosing in the therapy session. Level I content refers to the type of interaction generally reserved for the superficial contacts we have, for example, with store clerks. There is little risk of disclosing our inner thoughts and feelings in Level I self-disclosure. Level II content refers to the type of interaction we have with our acquaintances in the classroom and on the job. Again, many of these interactions are superficial, but they are extended over a longer period of time. Level III content refers to the type of interaction shared with our good friends. Usually a great deal of personal sharing occurs with those individuals with whom we invest large amounts of time. Often such friends help each other in times of crisis. Level IV content refers to those few persons who are our most trusted and close friends. These persons are the confidants to whom we entrust many of our hidden concerns. Level V content refers to "inner-circle" material, which is known only to us and to nobody else. Many individuals have a great deal of information stored here and others very little. It is a concern of school-counselors that some students have no one with whom they can share their Level IV and Level V material; consequently, the inner circles of these students are overloaded, in much the same way that an electrical circuit becomes overloaded.

Another way to look at the levels of self-disclosure characterizing a counseling interview would be to apply the Johari Window model to the process (Luft and Ingham 1963). The Johari Window consists of four frames representing different areas of self-knowledge: (1) information about self known to both self and others; (2) information about self known to self but not to others; (3) information about self known to others but not to self; (4) information about self known to nobody. Counseling, especially group counseling, is helpful in expanding self-awareness and thereby decreasing the size of the latter two frames in the model.

A final thought about self-disclosure raises the question of how much self-disclosure the counselor should do. This is definitely one of the major issues in the counseling profession. Both the pro and con sides of the issue have strong supporting points. Those favoring higher levels of counselor self-disclosure advance the following arguments:

1. If the counselor lays his cards on the table, the student will be likely to follow suit.
2. The student will be more relaxed and open if he realizes that the counselor has also experienced adjustment problems.
3. The student can benefit from listening to the method by which the counselor solved his or her problems.
4. The counselor should be a model for authenticity.

Those favoring lower levels of counselor self-disclosure advance the following arguments:

1. When you visit a physician you do not want to hear about his health problems. "Heal thyself" precedes healing others.
2. Counseling will become a "you tell me your problem and I'll tell you mine" if counselors disclose their problems to the student.
3. The delicate balance between objectivity and empathy would be disturbed if suddenly the student's concern becomes just like the one the counselor had when he was sixteen years old. That is, the individuality of the student's situation could be lost.

Jourard (1971) has described the relationship of self-disclosure and the group-leader as a matter of being in touch with one's own state of being. That is, the group session works best for Jourard when he (as the leader) discloses feelings, wishes, fantasies, and actions whenever these are relevant in an interaction between himself and others.

School-counselors must decide where they stand on the self-disclosure issue. How much self-disclosure they are willing to do would depend on how they view human nature and how their counseling method is shaped by this view. We believe that self-disclosure is most beneficial when it takes on a here-and-now focus—that is, when self-disclosure becomes an open and authentic expression of the counselor's and student's thoughts and feelings experienced at a particular moment in time. Self-disclosure, when examined in the here-and-now context, means much more than dredging up the dark secrets of the past.

## Expectations for the Counseling Interview

In 1959, Harper wrote a book entitled *Psychoanalysis and Psychotherapy: 36 systems.* Since that time several new approaches to counseling and psychotherapy have appeared in the counseling literature. In fact, there seems to be some truth to the saying that "theories are like people's children . . . it depends on whose they are!" Without entering the debate on which counseling approach is superior for all students at all times, we would prefer to examine some expectations shared by several counseling styles. School counseling offers the opportunity for the following counselor-student interactions:

1.  Listening in depth by the counselor to the feelings and content expressed by the student constitutes the first step. The counselor's first goal is to assist the student in telling his story. During the early part of the interview the counselor will help clarify the student's expectations for the counseling experience. Included will be a description of where the client is now in relation to where he would like to be. Later on in the interview, the student will be assisted in formulating a plan for reaching his goal.

2.  Evaluating present behavior patterns is the second part of the school-counseling experience. Unless the student evaluates his present behavior as not being helpful, he has no basis for making any changes in his day-to-day living pattern. The counselor's job is to assist the student in learning how to evaluate his own behaviors.

3.  Searching for alternative behaviors is the third phase of counseling. Once again, the counselor functions more as a facilitator than as a resource person. Responsibility for making decisions rests with the student.

4.  Commiting oneself to trying out a new behavior is the important fourth step in the counseling process. The counselor is usually interested in the student's ability to make and keep commitments as an index to his levels of independence and responsibility.

5.  Following up the student's commitments is the necessary final step in the counseling process. The follow-up process determines whether or not the above four stages need to be recycled and a new plan developed or modified from the old plan. The follow-up phase also offers opportunities for encouraging the growth in the student of ability to evaluate his or her behavior,

to generate alternative behaviors when needed, and to make and keep commitments.

## School Counseling Differs from Regular Conversation

We often classify our responses to students in counseling situations as being either counseling responses or "man-on-the-street" responses. Man-on-the-street responses resemble most ordinary types of conversation and should not be confused with good counseling technique. As examples of man-on-the-street responses, consider the responses to the following statement and select the one you would use: "Mr. Brown, I don't know what I'm going to do about algebra. I work at it all the time and still just can't seem to understand it."

*Responses:*
1. "You should try to plan your study time more carefully."
2. "If you don't get your head together on your algebra, you'll never get into college."
3. "Why don't you get someone to tutor you?"
4. "You're lucky that algebra is your only problem. I got an *F* in English and biology."
5. "It serves you right. You spend all your time shooting baskets. What did you expect might happen?"
6. "Why can't you seem to understand algebra?"
7. "Hey, do you know why some dogs make good mathematicians?"
8. "Don't worry, you've always been able to do math; you've got a high I.Q."
9. "I think you should apply the *SQ3R* method to studying your math. Tomorrow, I want you to discuss this with your teacher!"
10. "So what, nearly everybody in the class failed the test."
11. "I'm not surprised; you never did do your math well."
12. "Could it be that your failure to solve math problems is related to your failure to solve your own personal problems?"
13. "Look, you're a math dummy; you always have been and you always will be one!"

All of the above statements are of the man-on-the-street variety and all are better left out of the counseling interview. An examination of the above responses reveals that the student's feelings were disregarded entirely and, in some cases, even the content of the message was ignored.

The effective school-counselor will focus on both the feelings and the content of the student's message before proceeding to the planning stage of the interview. The effective school-counselor will refrain from judging, ridicule, psychoanalysis games, sympathy, probing, humorous distractions, praising, threatening, advising, debating, lecturing, and ordering—at least until the student has been able to express the feelings behind his concern. Even then, most of the above responses would be harmful to the counseling process unless used with selective care in specialized counseling approaches. For example, the rational-emotive approach developed by Ellis (1969) utilizes a lecture-type approach with considerable therapist-patient debate.

If the thirteen statements listed above are ineffective responses to the student's message, what would be an effective response? We think something similar to the following would be helpful: "Jim, it sounds as though you feel very discouraged about your algebra, because no matter what you have tried, nothing seems to work and you want to be able to find a way to understand it better."

This statement reflects Jim's feeling, his message, and his wish to work out a solution to his problem. With a little practice, most counselors can restate in a comfortable and authentic manner the student's feeling, his reason for it, and what he would like to have happen. Carkhuff (1973) presented the following teaching device for learning how to respond effectively to students. All you need to do is to fill in the blanks accurately:

You feel _____because _____

_____ ,

and you want _____ .

We do not mean to imply that you can conduct an entire counseling interview in one sentence. It may be necessary to use several such responses before the student agrees that his feelings and thoughts are fully understood. Once the accuracy of the feelings and thoughts has been established, the counseling interview should focus on developing a plan for helping the student attack his problem.

One weakness of the above approach is that school-counselors sometimes find it difficult to identify the correct feeling word. The process can be facilitated by first identifying the student's remark as expressing "pain" or "pleasure"; then finding a word that communicates the "pain" or "pleasure" and using it in your response. For example:

*Frank:*       "When all the guys play ball, sometimes I'm not cho-
            sen to be on a team."
            1.  Pain or Pleasure:                                   pain
            2.  Find a word which communicates the feeling:
                bored
                left-out
                isolated
                sad                                             left-out

*Counselor:*  "Frank, you sometimes feel left out of things, because
            you don't always get chosen to be on a team, and you
            want to find out how you can get the guys to choose
            you more often."


## SIGNIFICANT INFLUENCES ON THE DEVELOPMENT OF SCHOOL COUNSELING

School counseling, as a specialized skill, constitutes the major part of the formal school-guidance program (the counselor's noncounseling functions are discussed in another chapter). Formal guidance programs in schools are a product of the twentieth century. However, the philosophy and theory behind the guidance movement have been with us since the beginning of humankind. Men and women have always been concerned with their state of mental well-being as well as their physical health. Reports of mental disorders are found in the very earliest historical sources and in the literature of every period.

Humanity has always been concerned with the following functions served by counseling and the other guidance services:

1.  Educational problems.
2.  Vocational choices.
3.  Lack of skill.
4.  Conflict with self (indecision).
5.  Conflict with others (interpersonal relationships).
6.  Lack of self-knowledge.
7.  Lack of information about the environment.

As man became more civilized, it was natural for the tribe or community group to attempt to provide guidance to persons needing assistance. Many such community attempts to provide assistance to individual members are documented in cross-cultural studies of educational practices (ways of transmitting the culture), puberty rites,

and religious practices (Benedict 1946; Mead 1928). Early commun-
ity-guidance functions had the end-goal of survival for the individual
and for the group.

The pressures experienced by early man, striving to survive in
a hostile environment, required so much time and effort that there was
little leisure for speculation on the nature of personality and the roles
individuals should play. Choices made in this early age were directed
toward adaptation to the environment—that is, to staying alive and
eliminating as much daily stress as possible. Considerable faith was
placed in supernatural religious practices as a means of finding
security in a frightening universe. Human thought about life-choices
did not advance much beyond survival and superstition until the
Golden Age of Greece.

One of the first "guidance" publications, the *Republic*, was written by Plato (427-347 B.C.). In it he described his philosophy of education and career development. Recognizing human individuality,
Plato designed a society with an educational system to meet individual
needs. He employed a ladder system in education to determine how
an individual would serve humanity. The farther up the educational
ladder one went, the higher he would be placed in the work-force.
Career and educational counseling were done to the extent that people
were selected, placed, and evaluated in the various educational and
career stages. Individuals were evaluated by the criteria of how and
where they could best serve society. The ultimate goal of education
was to find the optimum role for everyone for the ultimate good of the
entire society—that is, the republic. The success of the republic
depended quite heavily on the selection process; the same probably
holds true for the success of school counseling as a profession.

Courses of study were regulated according to human developmental stages. Plato viewed education as a lifelong process, which
culminated in the placement of each individual at his highest level
of achievement. The potential governing body of the republic (the
philosopher-rulers) followed a sequential educational program. Up
to the age of seventeen, they studied literature, music, and elementary mathematics. From seventeen to twenty, they received physical
and military training only. Those between twenty and thirty studied
advanced mathematics, and those aged thirty to thirty-five studied
dialectics (the interrelationship of ideas). Between the ages of thirty-
five and fifty, the philosopher was to have practical experience in
minor offices and commands, both for the experience itself and as a
test of his ability to govern. From age fifty on he was to alternate between governing and studying—Plato made a good case for sabbati-
cal leave.

Plato also may have been among the first to recognize the rights of women. He wrote that women were to have the same tasks and opportunities as men. For this they were to receive the same mental, physical, and military training—in short, the same education and upbringing as men. In response to the argument that men and women should have different roles because of their different natures, Plato wrote that this was a superficial view, for some women are by nature more like some men than they are like other women. He concluded, therefore, that ability rather than sex (except for reproduction) should determine whether women would be philosopher-rulers, soldiers, or workers.

All individuals in Plato's plan would be given the opportunity to progress as far as they could. Those falling short would become the soldiers, farmers, and artisans. It is interesting to examine the place of mathematics in Plato's curriculum. He saw little practical value in mathematics except for the art of war; the main purpose of mathematics was to train the mind to think abstractly and to screen out the weaker minds in the program—functions now served, respectively, by statistics courses and the quantitative section of the Graduate Record Examination.

Plato did not base the educational and vocational selection and placement of individuals on the basis of intellect alone. He viewed some personality and character traits as important in addition to (not in place of) intellectual functioning. For example, philosopher-rulers were required to have a thorough knowledge and value orientation of what is good and just; they were not permitted to own property and were expected to function as friends of the citizens rather than as despots. The soldiers were required to have courage with knowledge, through conviction, of what to fear and what not to fear. As in the case of the philosopher-rulers, they would be supported by the producing class. The workers (farmers, merchants, and artisans) were expected to exhibit temperance and self-control along with the willingness to be governed by the upper class.

A review of Plato's *Republic* provides sufficient evidence that the guidance and counseling movement appeared in the history of humankind long before Francis Galton published *English Men of Science: Their Nature and Nurture* in 1874, or his later book, *Inquiries into the Human Faculty and Its Development* in 1883. Indeed, some writers cite the vocational-guidance activities of the Egyptians in 2400 B.C. as among the first on record. In any case, we believe that a true profession, which has come of age, has an origin and development that can be traced through their various stages. Because mature professions also have the benefit of enrichment from other disciplines, we will summarize some of the principal historical and interdisciplinary influences on the development of school counseling. Generally such influences may be grouped under innovations, government legislation, publications, professional organizations, training programs, professional standards, and cultural changes. However, since the school-counseling and guidance professions developed from the combined influences of several interrelated movements, a summary of the following movements is presented: (1) vocational guidance; (2) mental health; (3) psychological testing; and (4) progressive education; as well as (5) a survey of the history of school guidance itself.

### The Vocational-Guidance Movement

In 1881, Lysander Richards wrote a book entitled *Vocophy*, which treated the subject of vocational choice as it related to the study of phrenology. In 1884, President Andrew White of Cornell wrote a book entitled, *What Profession Shall I Choose and How Shall I Fit Myself for It?* White's book was written in response to the interest expressed by students and their parents. Apparently, there was much concern about the complexity of career-choice problems even before the beginning of the twentieth-century guidance movement. However, many people mark the real beginning of the vocational-guidance movement as being the posthumous publication in 1909 of *Choosing a Vocation* by Frank Parsons. In this book, Parsons presented a three-step counseling method for working with vocational-choice problems: (1) know the person; (2) know the world of work; (3) match the person with the job. Parsons's model, in addition to being logical and oversimplified, had implications for the training of counselors, the role of counselors, and the development of new assessment techniques. The counselor needed to be aware of his clients' strengths and weaknesses, likes and dislikes, past experiences, and special aptitudes. In addition, the counselor needed to have an in-depth knowledge of job requirements as well as knowledge of entry into the field. It might also be added that a Parsons-type counselor also needed to be familiar with the requirements for holding various jobs. Parsons's model also marks the beginning of trait-and-factor psychology. The counselor at the turn of the century had little to work with, outside his own subjective judgment, in evaluating his clients. In 1905, Parsons organized a vocational-guidance service and educational institute for both employed and unemployed persons in Boston. In 1908, the Vocation Bureau of Boston was opened; Frank Parsons served as its director and vocational counselor. Later on, in 1917, the bureau became part of the Division of Education at Harvard University, where it became the Bureau of Vocational Guidance. Meanwhile, in 1911, before becoming part of the Harvard scene, the Vocation Bureau began publishing the *Vocational Guidance News-Letter,* which began an evolutionary chain of three title and focus changes, culminating in the *Personnel and Guidance Journal.* In 1913, the National Vocational Guidance Association was founded.

Major federal legislation affecting the vocational guidance movement included:

1. 1913—the U.S. Department of Labor was organized.
2. 1917—the Smith-Hughes Act provided aid for vocational education.
3. 1918—the Vocational Rehabilitation Act provided rehabilitation for disabled veterans.
4. 1933—the Civilian Conservation Corps provided training and supervised employment for unemployed youth.
5. 1933—the Wagner-Peyser Act created the U.S. Employment Service.
6. 1935—the Works Progress Administration provided occupational opportunities for needy youth.
7. 1936—the George-Deen Act extended federal aid for vocational education in public schools.
8. 1943—Disabled Veterans Rehabilitation Act.
9. 1944—the G.I. Bill provided for extended educational and training benefits for military veterans.
10. 1946—the George-Barden Act provided support for vocational guidance.
11. 1954—Rehabilitation Amendments provided for a research and demonstration program to upgrade standards of training and practice.
12. 1962—the Manpower Development and Training Act provided for on-the-job vocational training for the unemployed and underemployed.
13. 1963—the National Vocational Education Act and the Vocational Amendment of 1968 provided for part-time employment for vocational-education students and supported research, training, and pilot programs for special vocational needs.
14. 1965—the Appalachian Regional Development Act provided for construction of vocational-educational facilities in the Appalachian region.

## The Mental Health Movement

In ancient times, mental illness was thought to be connected with possession by demons and evil spirits. Treatment consisted of magic and bizarre rituals designed to exorcise the demons. Some critics, observing various unorthodox present-day therapeutic practices, point out that we have not progressed much beyond the Dark Ages in our treatment of mental illness. The helpfulness of some of the orthodox methods, such as insulin shock, electric shock, and lobotomy, has also been questioned.

Many of the Dark Ages practices of treating mental illness continued through the Middle Ages and persisted well into the eighteenth century. Two eighteenth-century events in the mental-health movement are worth noting. Pinel is reported to have introduced understanding, kindness, and the development of interpersonal relationships as procedures in the asylums of eighteenth-century France. Mesmer's animal-magnetism theory grew out of his observation of the healing effects of hypnosis; his procedure was later referred to as mesmerism. Nonetheless, up to the end of the nineteenth century, considerable evidence shows that the mentally ill were still hanged, imprisoned, tortured, and treated as Satan's agents. They were chained and caged like wild animals and often left to die of starvation.

In 1896, Emil Kraeplin published a diagnostic classification of mental disorders, which served to alert the scientific community to the nature of mental dysfunction. During the same period, Adolf Meyer was publishing his theory about the mind-body relationship and Sigmund Freud was outlining his new approach to the understanding and treatment of neuroses.

Freud's early work with persons suffering from what was then known as hysterics marked the beginning of a new way to treat mental illness. In 1885, Freud, working with Charcot and Breuer in the use of hypnosis as a treatment for hysteria, discovered that patients suffering from hysteria were helped by "talking out" past emotional difficulties. Hypnosis was a way of helping the patient to recall past conflicts and trauma. Freud continued the "talking-out" process after bringing the patient back to the waking state. Frequently, Freud's patients experienced relief from their symptoms through the catharsis process. However, Freud concluded that additional methods were needed (these will be described in another chapter). The significance of Freud's work to the mental-health movement lies in his development of a verbal-therapy treatment. It might be added that Breuer reacted negatively to the increasingly obvious sexual content of his patients' early experiences and to the positive transference that his patients seemed to develop. Consequently, Breuer quit using the catharsis method and returned to traditional medical practice.

Two points become clear when reviewing the development of the mental-health movement: (1) social crisis seems to focus our attention on our personal welfare and on how we relate to others; (2) we probably think more seriously about our personal growth and adjustment when we are faced with personal conflicts or difficulties. Obviously, persons who are relatively free from intense pressure have little need to be concerned with mental health problems.

In 1908, Clifford Beers, describing his personal crisis and his experience as a patient in a mental hospital, wrote a book entitled, *A Mind That Found Itself.* A year later, in 1909, Beers founded the National Committee for Mental Hygiene. The mental health movement in the United States parallels the social crises surrounding both World Wars and the Depression years. The time-period surrounding World War I marked the development of the first large-scale personnel classification system for the United States Army. Yerkes and Scott followed the Parsons model of matching data about men with Army job descriptions. Two forms of an intelligence test (Army Alpha and Army Beta) were developed to test both literate and illiterate servicemen. World Wars I and II brought the appropriation of federal money for the rehabilitation of war veterans. The legislation for the years from 1918 to 1944, cited in the section on the vocational-guidance movement, reflects the influences of both wars and the Depression on the mental health movement.

The National Mental Health Act, enacted by Congress in 1946, established the National Institute of Mental Health, which administers funds for research and training. In 1950 the National Association for Mental Health was formed by the merger of the three major mental health organizations: the National Committee for Mental Hygiene, the National Mental Health Foundation, and the National Psychiatric Foundation.

## The Psychological-Testing Movement

The five movements influencing the development of school counseling have considerable interrelatedness. The psychological-testing movement is no exception. We have already reviewed the role of testing in the vocational-guidance and mental-health movements. Additionally, we will summarize some of the other effects of test development on school counseling and guidance.

Alfred Binet in 1904 constructed a test for distinguishing between normal and subnormal performance on a series of verbal and nonverbal tasks. His primary objective was to identify children who needed special educational programs. Unfortunately, these children were referred to as feeble-minded. In 1905, Terman translated the Binet test for use in the United States. The development of the Army General Classification Test, discussed in the preceding section, spurred the use and construction of multiple-aptitude tests. The National Defense Education Act (Title V-A) of 1958 provided funds for the establishment of testing programs in both private and public schools.

Parsons's original model for vocational counseling provided the impetus for the start of the testing movement. As we mentioned above, his model called for the identification of personal traits and abilities, which would then be matched with a vocation requiring those characteristics. During Parsons's time, no instruments were available for measuring aptitudes, interests, abilities, and self-concepts. Without means for measuring personal traits, Parsons's three-stage process was not functional. Therefore, the opportunity for test development was wide open. Up until 1930, test construction and the measurement of human traits was the primary focus of American psychology. The testing movement also marked the move away from a total dependence on a philosophical basis for guidance to a more scientific framework.

## The Progressive-Education Movement

The focus of the progressive-education movement was directed to the primary role and importance of the learner in the teaching-learning process. John Dewey and his pragmatic philosophy provided considerable direction for the movement, which emphasized school as a preparation for life. Perhaps the major contribution of the movement was to motivate educators to concern themselves with the total development of the child.

## Developments in the School-Counseling and Guidance Movement

Between the years 1914 and 1918, city-wide school-guidance programs were started in the following cities: Cincinnati, Lincoln, Oakland, Boston, Philadelphia, Pittsburgh, Atlanta, Seattle, and Providence. In 1932, John Brewer's book, *Education as Guidance*, pointed out the importance of making school counseling and guidance an integral part of the education process. In 1942, Carl Rogers published *Counseling and Psychotherapy*, which outlined a new counseling approach. Rogers's method emphasized the positive

growth forces of all people with the counselor taking the role of helping the person help himself. Rogers's approach was referred to as a
nondirective approach in that the counselor did a lot of listening,
reflecting, and clarifying and very little sermonizing, lecturing, and
advice-giving.

In 1951, the American Personnel and Guidance Association was
formed. In 1957, the Russians were successful in launching *Sputnik,*
the first unmanned space flight. Americans suddenly became concerned about the quality of their country's educational system, and
as a result the National Defense Education Acts were passed as a
means for identifying and developing the potential of the gifted among
our youth. Of the ten titles in the Act, one (Title V) was reserved for
school counseling and guidance. Part of the NDEA support was
directed toward school testing programs and the other part toward
training institutes for counselor trainees and for experienced counselors. In 1959, in *The American High School Today,* James Conant
recommended the expansion of counseling and guidance services in
the schools. Unfortunately, his recommended ratio of one counselor
for every three hundred students became etched in stone for a period
of time. Since then, some school systems have shown a willingness
to consider a lower counselor-student ratio. In 1960 the White House
Conference on Children and Youth made a plea for strengthening
the vocational-guidance, informational-service, and placement-
service aspects of the total school-counseling and guidance program.

Since this 1960 time-period, school counseling and guidance
have made significant gains. Training programs for counselors and
support personnel are being funded under the Education Professions Development Act. Possibly the most promising of the federally
funded guidance programs are the elementary-school guidance programs receiving support from Title III of the Elementary and Secondary Education Act. With the recent emphasis on accountability,
or on showing proof of your worth, the ESEA programs are designed
to meet specified measurable objectives. The Robertson County
Elementary School Guidance Project,* encompassing seven separate
programs across the State of Tennessee, is presently providing an
excellent model of what these ESEA projects can accomplish.

The current state of the American Personnel and Guidance Association reveals that considerable progress has taken place since its
founding in 1951. Presently there are nine divisions in APGA: (1)

*Mrs. Bettye Alley is director of the project. Those wishing information about the
project may write to her at Robertson County Board of Education, 22nd and Wood-
lawn Street, Springfield, Tenn., 37172.

Association for Counselor Education and Supervision (ACES), (2) American School Counselor Association (ASCA), (3) National Vocational Guidance Association (NVGA), (4) American Rehabilitation Counseling Association (ARCA), (5) National Employment Counselors Association (NECA), (6) Association for Measurement and Evaluation of Guidance (AMEG), (7) Student Personnel Association for Teacher Education (SPATE), (8) American College Personnel Association (ACPA), and (9) Association for Non-White Concerns in Personnel and Guidance (ANWC).

Some counselors also belong to Division 17 of the American Psychological Association, the Division of Counseling Psychology. Division 17, claiming one of the largest memberships of the APA branches, has been active in promoting counseling research, ethics, and training standards.

Numerous professional journals have sprung from the many counseling-related organizations. These include the *Journal of Counseling Psychology*, the *School Counselor*, *Elementary School Guidance and Counseling*, *Counselor Education and Supervision*, *Vocational Guidance Quarterly*, *American Psychologist*, and *Personnel and Guidance Journal*.

The present trend in the continuing development of school counseling is toward career education. To most experienced counselors, the term *career education* is a new label for what effective school-counselors have been doing for years—for example, developing activities designed to increase self-concept, career awareness, and personal awareness of strengths, interests, and values.

## INTERDISCIPLINARY INFLUENCES ON SCHOOL COUNSELING

Some of the interdisciplinary influences on school counseling are evident in the five movements examined in the preceding sections. Without a doubt, the influence of psychiatry and psychology on school counseling has been paramount. The techniques and methods used by counselors had their origins in these two fields. Newer counseling methods are largely adaptations from some of the classical approaches to psychological treatment. Information on human motivation, growth and development, and cognitive functioning also comes from psychology.

Philosophy and religion have also been influential in helping school-counselors come to terms with human nature. Only with a clear conception of human nature can a school-counselor decide which counseling methods are both ethical and helpful. The influence of religion on school counseling may come from the fact that the counseling profession seems to attract so many former seminarians.

The study of economics has influenced school counseling by contributing to an understanding of people as economic beings existing in some type of economic system and expected to produce and consume goods and services. It is important that school-counselors be aware of economic motivations and how such motivations affect all of our lives.

The contribution of political science to school counseling largely falls into the category of an understanding of the nature of power in society. How does one attain and exercise power? What role does personal decision-making play in any particular political system? These are the questions posed to the discipline of political science by school-counselors interested in helping students become better problem-solvers.

Sociology and anthropology have provided helpful information for school-counselors regarding social-class cultural roles, cultural lag, cultural patterns, status motivation, and "hidden persuaders." Perhaps the most helpful influence of these two related disciplines has been the development of awareness of the individual differences and similarities deriving from the many cultures and subcultures represented in the population of even one school.

Knowledge of mathematics enables the school-counselor to calculate and interpret measurement data. The natural sciences provide clues on human development, and the humanities on the potential of human growth and development. In short, school-counselors are the best prepared to do their job if they have a thorough liberal arts background.

## REFERENCES

Benedict, R. 1946. *Patterns of Culture*. New York: Mentor Books.

Blocher, D. 1966. *Developmental Counseling*. New York: Ronald Press.

Carkhuff, R. 1969. *Helping and Human Relations*. 2 vols. New York: Holt, Rinehart & Winston.

———. 1973. "Human Achievement, Educational Achievement, Career Achievement: Essential Ingredients of Elementary School Guidance." Paper presented at Second Annual National Elementary School Guidance Conference, March 30, 1973, at Louisville, Kentucky.

Conant, J. 1959. *The American High School Today*. New York: McGraw-Hill.

Ellis, A. 1969. "Teaching Emotional Education in the Classroom." *School Health Review* 1:10-13.

Gelatt, H.; Varenhorst, B.; and Carey, R. 1972. *Deciding.* New York: College Entrance Examination Board.

Greenwood, E. 1962. "Attributes of a Profession." *Social Work.* 2:45-55.

Harper, R. 1954. *Psychoanalysis and Psychotherapy: 36 Systems.* Englewood Cliffs, N.J.: Prentice-Hall.

Jourard, S. 1971. *The Transparent Self.* 2d ed. New York: Van Nostrand Reinhold.

Lazarus, A. 1969. "The Inner Circle Strategy: Identifying Crucial Problems." In *Behavioral Counseling: Cases and Techniques,* ed. J. Krumboltz and C. Thoresen. New York: Holt, Rinehart, & Winston.

Luft, J., and Ingham, H. 1963. "The Johari Window: A Graphic Model of Awareness in Interpersonal Relations." *Group Processes: An Introduction to Group Dynamics.* Palo Alto, Calif.: National Press Books.

Maslow, A. 1970. *Motivation and Personality.* New York: Harper & Row.

Mead, M. 1928. *Coming of Age in Samoa.* New York: William Morrow.

Pepinsky, H., and Pepinsky, P. 1954. *Counseling: Theory and Practice.* New York: Ronald Press.

Peters, H., and Farwell, G. 1967. *Guidance: A Developmental Approach.* 2d ed. Chicago: Rand McNally.

Rogers, C. 1942. *Counseling and Psychotherapy.* Boston: Houghton Mifflin.

Schofield, W. 1964. *Psychotherapy: The Purchase of Friendship.* Englewood Cliffs, N.J.: Prentice-Hall.

Thompson, C. 1969. "The Secondary School Counselor's Ideal Client." *Journal of Counseling Psychology,* 16:69-74.

Thompson, C., and Poppen, W. 1972. *For Those Who Care: Ways of Relating to Youth.* Columbus: Charles E. Merrill.

Toffler, A. 1970. *Future Shock.* New York: Random House.

Williamson, E. 1950. *Counseling Adolescents.* New York: McGraw-Hill.

CHAPTER 2

# Contemporary Theories of School Counseling

## PSYCHOANALYSIS

### Definition

Psychoanalysis, founded by Sigmund Freud, is a method of psychological treatment that examines past causes for present behavior. The focus is on how the individual adjusted to the various conflicts in his development. For example, one psychoanalytic technique is to interpret the individual's present behavior in the light of how he adjusted to the stress caused by weaning, toilet training, relationships with parents, and puberty. Freud viewed his method as a procedure for investigating parts of the human mental process that were inaccessible in any other way. To Freud, the key to treating mental disorders was to reach the unconscious aspects of the individual's mental processes.

### View of Human Nature

Freud viewed human beings as victims of unconscious determinants, which motivate them to seek immediate fulfillment of basic needs. As such, human beings were seen in a negative light as often tending to act irrationally and impulsively to satisfy selfish interests. From the above, it is easy to conclude that Freud's view of human beings was pessimistic. However, it should be remembered that Freud formulated his ideas on the basis of extended contacts with neurotics who had lost their ability to be self-directing persons.

Freud considered the human individual to be an animal handicapped by having to chose ways to meet his personal needs. Three aspects of the human personality were postulated: (1) the *id*—the individual's specific drives emerging from an immediate attempt to

31

meet physical needs—it also provides the energy of the mind (libid-inal and aggressive energy); (2) the *superego*—the individual's conscience or inner voice, which dictates a lot of "shoulds" and "should nots" about the person's behavior—because they are both extreme in their influences, the id and superego are both illogical and potentially harmful if one allows his life to be governed by either; (3) the *ego*, which mediates the battle between the id and superego, maintaining a state of balance between itself and the other two aspects of personality—while it is the conscious and logical self of the person, the ego is not tied down to reality.

Various defense mechanisms are employed by the ego to satisfy the demands of the id and superego. For example, sublimation allows the individual to meet the basic needs of the id while still satisfying the demands of the conscience (superego). Meat-cutters and surgeons may be examples of individuals who have sublimated their aggres-sive drives into socially approved activities. Statements like the pre-ceding one do not serve to make psychoanalytic theory popular among some groups of people, such as meat-cutters and surgeons. Other defense mechanisms used by the ego when personal goals are blocked include: rationalization (sour grapes), projection (laying your weaknesses or motives on someone else), denial ("it doesn't exist"), reaction formation (accentuate the opposite), introjection (imitation of or identification with someone else), repression (forget it), and regression (retreat to comfortable stage).

Freud's theory (1949) argued that the life-force (eros) or libido (which was primarily sexual in nature) was directed toward the search for pleasure. This life-force was the energy that propelled the indi-vidual through each developmental stage, culminating in sexual maturity. The stages are: (1) oral (age 0-1 year), (2) anal (age 1-3 years), (3) phallic (age 3-7 years), (4) latency (age 7-13 years), and (5) genital (age 12-14 years).

Freud developed six hypotheses about human nature:

1. Psychic determinism—all thoughts and actions are caused by some preceding event.
2. Unconscious mental processes hold the key to human motiva-tion. (This idea, combined with the first hypothesis, is the basis of the psychoanalytic view of human nature: all behavior is caused and the cause generally will be found in unconscious mental processes.)
3. Bisexuality—all human beings have some inclination toward the tendencies of the opposite sex. Freud believed that guilt

and anxiety regarding bisexuality were harbored in the unconscious mental processes.

4. Bipolarity or ambivalence of emotions—positive feelings are
   usually accompanied by some negative feelings, and vice versa.
   However, one or another type of reaction is usually repressed
   in the unconscious, and consequently the individual is only
   aware of one aspect of his emotional reaction.
5. Displacement function—this process may be described as the
   representation of a part by the whole or of the whole by a part.
   For example, a bad experience with a perceived authority-figure
   may be generalized to all persons in positions of authority.
6. Sublimation—the redirection of sexual energy into nonsexual
   activities of an aesthetic or utilitarian nature that satisfy social
   and personal standards of approval. Freud believed sublimation to be the force behind the development of civilization.

## Method of Counseling

The primary purpose of psychoanalytic counseling is to release
the causal material repressed in the unconscious parts of the mental
process. In order to accomplish this task, the therapist, remaining out
of the patient's sight, sits behind the couch on which the patient is
reclining. In such an objective posture, the therapist reveals very
little, if anything, of his own inner world to the patient. The patient
is encouraged to relax and relate whatever comes into his mind, no
matter how irrelevant or personal his thoughts may be. A main purpose of the counseling process is directed toward weakening both
the resistances that shut off the person's awareness of himself and
the discrepancies between his and others' views of himself. The
analyst uses free association, dream analysis, parapraxis (for example,
slips of the tongue), and humor analysis as a beginning for looking
into the unconscious material. The psychoanalytic setting with the
free-association technique is highly conducive to the development
of transference—the process in which the patient displaces to the
therapist the love or hatred unconsciously attached to a significant
person in his past. Hopefully, through achieving insight into the
reasons for his present behavior pattern, the patient will be able to
replace his self-defeating behaviors with productive ones.

## Counseling Goals

In addition to developing insight, it is helpful if the patient can free himself from the repressions of his early childhood and replace these with higher levels of rational thought from the superego. The main purpose of treatment is the unification and strengthening of the ego to enable the person to expend the energy heretofore wasted on internal conflicts on developing his highest potential. Symptom-removal is generally achieved as a by-product of the analysis.

Psychoanalysis was included in this book because some contemporary counseling approaches borrow heavily from it, others lightly, and still others were established as reactions against it. There are some additional reasons for the school-counselor to know psychoanalytic theory and practice:

1. Child-rearing and teaching practices significantly affect the way children develop.
2. Children pass through different stages of development, with mastery of tasks of increasing difficulty required in each succeeding stage.
3. Persons sometimes do seem to be motivated by unconscious processes or at least by impulses of which they are not fully aware.
4. The counseling interview offers a setting in which students may examine the nature and causes of their anxieties.
5. The counselor might do well to withhold judgmental statements conveying moralizing messages.
6. A knowledge of psychoanalytic theory should help school-counselors to determine what their limitations are in counseling severely disturbed children and adolescents.

## INDIVIDUAL PSYCHOLOGY

### Definition

Individual psychology is the system of psychotherapy developed by Alfred Adler (1969). Until his recent death, Rudolph Dreikurs (1968) was the leading proponent of individual psychology. The underlying idea of the system is that behavior is controlled by attempts, generally unwitting, to compensate for feelings of inferiority. Adler rejected Freud's idea that the libido and the will to pleasure are the main causes of behavior in favor of the idea that the search for power determines human actions and development. With the primary focus on the will to power, development in the Adlerian system of individual psychology may be viewed as a process of becoming less inferior. However, in recent years Adlerian psychologists have viewed the real motivating power as the desire to belong—a social interest.

## View of Human Nature

Adler brought the concept of free will and self-determinism to psychology at a time when there was no room for this concept, which views human beings as free to make choices and to select their own life-styles. With the prime motivation of helping the patient to find his place in his family or group, Adlerian psychologists look for patterns of behavior. For example, when the quest for personal need-fulfillment is frustrated (especially the need to belong), people resort to four ways of misbehaving in order to achieve their goals: (1) attention-getting, (2) power-struggling, (3) revenge-seeking, and (4) displaying inadequacy. The goals of misbehavior have a developmental nature. If attention-getting doesn't work, the person may resort to power-struggling, and so forth.

Another facet of human nature in the Adlerian system is the position a person occupies in his childhood family constellation. First-born children have certain typical characteristics, such as being high-achievers and perfectionistic. Second-born children are thought to avoid the tremendous pressure of competing with number-one by selecting their own "thing" by which to find their place. Many second-borns choose to be more outgoing and sociable than their older sibling. Third-born children may relish and take advantage of everyone by being the family baby even through the adult years if everyone else will play the game.

## Method of Counseling

Most practitioners of the Adlerian method seem to function best as consultants to parents and teachers. Using a teleo-analytic approach—that is, examining the purposes and consequences of behavior—the consultant suggests ways the adult can manage the particular goal of misbehavior the child is striving to meet. For example, the attention-getter should not get attention for his annoying behavior. Another consultant-type function is to examine with the parents how the child's birth-order may be affecting his behavior. A favorite method of Adlerians is to do a demonstration family-counseling session in front of a group of parents experiencing similar family problems. The goal is for each parent to generalize the analysis and suggestions to his own family. Group discussions have long been a part of the system. The focus of such group discussions remains on the purposiveness of behavior, which is not to be confused with antecedent causes of behavior.

A favorite technique of Adlerian psychologists is to use a series of "could it be" questions when counseling children and adolescents. For example, "Could it be that you want me to notice you?" or "Could it be that you want to keep me busy with you?" In answer to the question, "How do you know which goal of misbehavior is being attained?" the Adlerians recommend paying attention to your inner feelings. For example, on the form below, match the feelings you have with the goal of misbehavior your child is probably after. (If you wish, you may also match the most helpful intervention technique with the appropriate misbehavior goal.)

*Goals of Misbehavior* (Your child's behavior)

_____ _____1. Attention-Getting
_____ _____2. Power-Struggling
_____ _____3. Revenge-Seeking
_____ _____4. Display of Inadequacy

| *Your Feelings* | *What You Can Do* |
| --- | --- |
| a. hurt | e. refuse to fight |
| b. helpless | f. convince child he is liked—do group counseling |
| c. annoyed | g. encourage |
| d. threatened | h. ignore the behavior |

*Answers*

1. *c & h*
2. *d & e*
3. *a & f*
4. *b & g*

**Counseling Goals**

The main counseling goal of Adlerian psychology is to decrease feelings of inferiority by helping persons find new and "approved" ways of finding their places in their families or groups. Increasing social interest and social skills are also primary counseling goals. Both of these outcomes would serve to enhance the person's self-concept. Redirection of goal orientation from counter-productive misbehavior to helpful, need-fulfilling behavior is also a common counseling goal for Adlerians. Since the method is a teaching approach, the test you just finished is quite apropos for individual psychology.

## LOGOTHERAPY

### Definition

With psychoanalysis and individual psychology respectively constituting the first and second Viennese schools of psychotherapy, we have the third Viennese school in Viktor Frankl's logotherapy. Freud based his theory on the will to pleasure and Adler based his on the will to power. Frankl (1962) introduced still a third concept: the will to meaning in life. Adopting the philosopher Nietzsche's statement, "He who has a why to live for, can bear almost any how," Frankl constructed his approach around ways to help persons discover the meaning in their own lives. The term *logos*, which he adopted as the name for his theory, translates as "meaning" and "valuing." Frankl survived a four-year imprisonment in German concentration camps during World War II. Living through this experience, and managing to find meaning in it, despite the fact that his mother, father, wife, and brother all perished in the death camps, provided the basis for his theory. His writings on it have become very popular.

### View of Human Nature

Frankl describes three characteristics of human existence: (1) human beings are unities with three dimensions: physical, psychological, and spiritual; (2) human beings have freedom in spite of instincts, inherited dispositions, and environment; (3) human beings have the responsibility for finding meaning in their lives. We alone determine the meaning of our existence and must accept ultimate responsibility for our lives. Since humankind was denied some of the basic animal instincts that make animal behavior an automatic process, we have to make choices and decisions.

### Method of Counseling

Frankl employs considerable amounts of evangelizing and verbal persuasion in his method of trying to help others find meaning in their lives. Sometimes he refers to this as filling the existential vacuum.

Frankl believes that personal existential vacuums (boredom, lack of purpose in life, frustration) can be filled in three ways:

1. By doing a deed—achievement.
2. By experiencing a value—experiencing something of beauty or experiencing someone through love.
3. By suffering—finding meaning in unavoidable suffering. Suffering can have meaning if it changes you for the better. Suffering is a key concept in Frankl's system. He believes that failure to find meaning in suffering and death is a failure to find meaning in life because those two experiences are parts of life.

Frankl employs specific counseling techniques for symptom relief. Two such techniques are paradoxical intention and de-reflection. Paradoxical intention is a process for defeating anticipatory anxiety, which thrives in an existential vacuum. Fill the vacuum and you defeat anticipatory anxiety because you have no time to sit around and worry about "what might happen if." As a short-cut to filling the vacuum, the counselor may employ the paradoxical-intention technique of asking the person to practice the symptom of his fear. For example, practice passing out or blushing. By adding humor to the situation, the counselor is generally successful in getting the student to laugh at and ridicule his symptoms. Of course, when one does try to pass out or tries to set a record for staying awake, the opposite usually happens. The de-reflection technique focuses the individual's attention away from himself so that he can ignore his neurosis. A symptom evokes a phobia and a phobia evokes a symptom, and on and on. Fear tends to make come true precisely that of which one is afraid. The de-reflection method is geared to defeat hyperintention (a fear of not being able to meet the demands of others). In other words, de-reflection helps to destroy "perceived expectations of others." For example, in a case of test anxiety, the counselor can order the student not to make a passing grade on any of his next five tests. Provided that the student is really capable of performing better, he will probably do so with the pressure removed.

### Counseling Goals

The main goal of logotherapy is to find meaning in one's life. To do this, life plans, as well as long- and short-term planning, are considered to be guards against a planless existence. Attacks will be launched on the fatalistic attitude of "being a victim of my environment rather than a controller of my life." Attention is also directed toward the balance one gives to his own concerns in relation to those of others. In other words, does the individual prefer to lose himself in the masses or does he go overboard in the other direction and ignore everyone else's thoughts and feelings?

## REALITY THERAPY

### Definition

Reality therapy, as developed by William Glasser (1965), stresses how the three R's of *reality, responsibility,* and *right and wrong* relate to a person's life situation. The focus of reality is directed toward the individual's current behavior. Past behavior, viewed as something unalterable, is not given much consideration or attention in the counseling process. In fact, the system of reality therapy seems to have developed as a reaction against many of the practices of psychoanalysis. Glasser (1965) summarizes the six presuppositions of conventional psychoanalysis:

1. The reality of mental illness.
2. Reconstructive exploration of the patient's past.
3. Transference.
4. An unconscious, which must be plumbed.
5. Interpretation rather than evaluation of behavior.
6. Change occurs through insight and permissiveness.

Glasser's system of reality therapy attacks these main tenets of psychoanalytic theory head-on:

1. The concept of mental illness is not used. People get sick because they behave irresponsibly; that is, they attempt to meet their needs at someone else's expense.
2. The counselor works with the present behavior of his students. The past history of his students is not given much attention in the counseling process.
3. The counselor relates to the students as himself and does not attempt to assume the role of a transference figure.
4. The counselor does not look for unconscious conflicts and the reasons or excuses for them. The focus is on having the student evaluate but not excuse his own behavior.
5. The counselor faces the issue of right and wrong with his students. The issue of right and wrong concerns the degree of

helpfulness of the student's behavior. Who was helped? How were they helped? These are two important questions raised in the process.

6. Counseling is really re-education or a teaching-learning situation in which students learn better ways to fulfill their needs.

**View of Human Nature**

Practitioners of reality therapy acknowledge the influence of heredity and environment on humankind, but they reject the deterministic view of man as a helpless victim of these forces. Rather, the reality-therapy philosophy holds to an existential view of humankind, which makes each individual responsible for his own decisions and behavior.

Glasser, agreeing with Maslow (1970), believes that we have two primary needs above and beyond survival. These are the needs to give and receive love and to feel worthwhile. Generally the two needs seem to run well together. People who give and receive love generally feel worthwhile, and vice versa. The key to feeling worthwhile is first to evaluate your behavior and then to change it if it falls below the standards you have set for yourself.

In contrast to the Freudian view that psychological disorders arise when culture (superego) conflicts with physiological and pleasure needs (id), Glasser believes that such disorders are due to an inability to fulfill one's needs. Rather than face their inability to satisfy their needs, some persons deny the reality of the world around them by making excuses for their behavior. With responsibility defined as the ability to fill one's needs without infringing on the rights of others, or without depriving others of the opportunity to fill theirs, the responsible person becomes the mentally healthy person in the system of reality therapy.

**Method of Counseling**

School-counselors using reality therapy would follow three steps in the counseling process: (1) Become actively involved with the students. Very little can be accomplished until the students believe that the counselor really cares about them. The best way to establish an effective counseling relationship is through reacting honestly to your students. One way to begin the relationship may be to say that you will continue to see the student until he no longer needs to see you. Once again, the best way to build most relationships is through active listening (see Chapter 1). (2) With the relationship established, the counselor will be in a position to reject the student's behavior without making the student feel personally rejected. (3) The counselor can begin the re-education program, which essentially involves seven substeps outlined by Glasser (1972):

1. Maintain involvement with the student.
2. Ask the student to examine his current behaviors (What are you doing?).
3. Ask the student to evaluate his current behaviors (How is it helping?).
4. If the student's current behavior is not working, ask him to think of alternative plans (What could you be doing that would help you the most?).
5. Ask the student to develop a plan and make a commitment to try it out (Which alternative will you try and when?).
6. Accept no excuses (never ask *why* when misbehavior is involved).
7. Administer no punishment (punishment breaks student trust and destroys involvement). The system of logical consequences, which relates what one does to the consequences of his behavior, has far more validity than irrational punishment.

Counselors utilizing reality therapy on a one-to-one basis also find it helpful in large and small group-counseling sessions. As is the case in one-to-one-counseling, the counselor does not sit in judgment on what the students say and do. Behavior changes when the individual makes his own negative evaluation of what he is doing.

## Counseling Goals

The primary goal of reality therapy is to assist students in finding their reality by overcoming loneliness through involvement and by breaking the cycle of personal failure through a series of successes. Of course, the main goal is to teach students ways to meet their needs more effectively and thereby make them more responsible and, hence, mentally healthy persons.

## CLIENT-CENTERED COUNSELING

### Definition

Client-centered counseling, developed by Carl Rogers (1951), is based on the beliefs that problems originate from emotional blocks or conflicts, and that people already have the necessary objective knowledge for deciding what needs to be done about their problems. Therefore, the task of the client-centered counselor is to establish a warm and accepting relationship in which the student feels free to let himself be known. As trust builds between counselor and student, the counselor is able, through empathic understanding, to perceive the world as the student sees it and also how the student views himself in his world. These empathic perceptions are communicated to the student in a way that assists him in clarifying the relationship between his thoughts and feelings. Client-centered counseling has often been called the first truly American school of counseling.

### View of Human Nature

The client-centered approach to counseling is based on a very positive view of human nature. Client-centered counseling has also been identified with third-force psychology (the other two forces being psychoanalysis and behaviorism), humanistic psychology, and existential psychology. All of these approaches have the common factor of holding the following positive views of humankind:

1. People are socialized, forward-moving, rational, and realistic —striving to become all that they can become. The human organism strives to provide more than a maintenance function; it seeks to actualize and enhance the living experience.
2. Human potential varies in degree, but each person has the power to make helpful changes in his life.
3. Being naturally autonomous, people should be given opportunities to develop and exercise their abilities to direct their own lives.
4. People are able to make constructive decisions if they are given an opportunity to view their concerns objectively in a relaxed setting free from criticism and threat.
5. People are basically trustworthy and constructive; that is, the deepest layer of the human personality is positive.

### Method of Counseling

Believing that the good in people will emerge if given a chance, the client-centered counselor will refrain from prescribing, giving solutions, giving advice, lecturing, and nagging. Instead, the method utilizes (1) active listening, (2) reflection of feelings and thoughts, (3) clarification, and (4) general or open leads that facilitate the client's self-exploration.

Responsibility for the interview is largely with the client. What better way exists to get the client back on the road to taking responsibility? In fact, what better way exists to further the client's development of independence? The client is responsible for the interview content. Almost never will new material be introduced by the client-centered counselor. Naturally, the counselor will refrain from making any decisions for the client.

Catharsis occurs in client-centered therapy, but is more of an emotional release of present feelings than a dredging up of the traumas of early childhood. Present adjustment certainly has precedence over trying to resolve an unalterable past.

Client-centered counselors have little use for diagnostic labels and for various testing devices and procedures that have been developed as counseling aids. Once again, the counseling focus is based on an "emergence" theory of human functioning: the good will out.

In summary, then, psychological treatment administered according to client-centered principles involves freeing the client to become himself; this is dependent on the following necessary conditions of therapy: the counselor's attitude of positive regard, genuineness, and empathic understanding.

Carkhuff (1973) has been successful in rating the quality of empathy expressed by counselors in each of their responses to students. The latest rating system, comprising five levels of empathy, has been helpful in both researching and explaining what the client-centered counselor does. For example, an effective counselor will be successful in helping students go through a three-step process of identifying: (1) where they are, (2) where they would like to be in relation to where they are, and (3) a plan for getting from (1) to (2). A level-one rating on the Carkhuff scale means that the counselor-response only keyed in on step (2). A level-three rating means that the response identified step (1) only. A level-four response means that the counselor identified steps (1) and (2), and a level-five response means that the counselor was successful in identifying all three steps.

The 1970s have found Rogers concentrating more on group therapy than on individual therapy. Observation of Rogers's groups reveals that he proceeds with groups in much the same way he does with individuals.

**Counseling Goals**

The outcome for the client-centered counselor would approximate Rogers's observations and expectations for both individuals and groups (1951; 1970). It is expected that:

1. During the latter part of counseling, the students' conversation will include an increased discussion of plans, behavioral steps to be undertaken, and the outcomes of these steps.
2. An examination of all references to current behavior will indicate that there is a change from relatively immature behavior to relatively mature behavior during the course of the interviews.
3. There will be a decrease in current defensive behaviors and a greater awareness of those defensive behaviors which are present.
4. The student will show an increased tolerance for frustration.
5. One behavioral outcome of client-centered counseling will be improved functioning in life-tasks: for example, improvement in reading on the part of school children or improvement in adjustment to job-training and job-performance on the part of adults.

## BEHAVIORAL COUNSELING

### Definition

Behavioral counseling, as developed by Skinner and Lindsley (1954), Eysenck (1964), Wolpe (1969), Krasner and Ullman (1965), Krumboltz and Thoresen (1969), and others, is the use of experimentally established principles of learning for the purpose of changing maladaptive behavior.

### View of Human Nature

People are viewed as being neither innately good nor innately bad. At the beginning of their lives they are like Locke's *tabula rasa* upon which nothing has been stamped. As reactive beings, they react to environmental stimuli and consequently are largely products of their environment. Heredity does play an important part in human development, but since you can change environment more easily than you can change heredity, the focus of behavioral counseling is on changing behavior through changing the environment—including the environment in the counseling interview.

People learn patterns of behavior because various actions and reactions are accompanied or followed by a satisfying condition and are consequently stamped-in to be repeated at a later date. A pattern of behavior is repeated as long as the payoff is repeated. The reinforcement process used in behavioral counseling is based on human needs. A need exists when survival of the organism is not facilitated; therefore, the organism acts in such a way as to reduce these needs. Reinforcement, being based on need reduction, is the instrumental factor in the counseling-learning process.

## Method of Counseling

Behavioral counseling views counseling as re-education or re-learning. Learning is defined as the process by which a person's present behavior is modified because of some prior activity. Since such modifications can be either good or bad, mental illness and emotional disturbance are considered to be the result of unfavorable learning experiences. Counseling thus becomes a process of re-education, unlearning, or counter-conditioning. Some self-defeating behaviors are repeated because they bring immediate anxiety-reduction (e.g., smoking) although they may be bad in the long run. Another example would be the shy student who withdraws.

On the assumption that behavior is a function of its antecedents and, consequently, that behavior is predictable, behavioral counseling consists of manipulating and controlling antecedents. Another assumption is that fear and anxiety (phobic reactions) are learned emotional reactions to once neutral stimuli, which were presented a number of times together with noxious stimuli. For example, Albert began to fear white, furry objects because each time he was presented with one he also heard a loud gong. Therefore, much of the behavioral-counseling process is directed toward extinguishing learned responses; four techniques are suggested:

1. Desensitization. This is a process of adaptation where the stimulus is presented very weakly and then gradually increased until the student can handle it without anxiety. For example, in cases of acrophobia, the student could begin the stimulus hierarchy by simply thinking about looking out a first-story window and gradually progresses to actually looking out a first-story window, and so on.
2. Internal inhibition. This is inhibitory conditioning where the stimulus is continually presented at very short intervals. This is also called massing of trials, especially when the process

leads to sufficient fatigue in the student that he or she stops the response. For example, many people fear snakes because the long time-lapse between seeing snakes actually reinforces the fear response.

3. Counter-conditioning. This is the process of pairing a pleasant stimulus with a noxious or unpleasant stimulus. For example, pairing chocolate candy with sitting in an automobile (the feared object).

4. Aversion therapy. This process involves pairing something like an electric shock or rubber-band snap on the wrist with the maladaptive response. For example, the smoker could be wired to receive a weak electric shock each time he bent his smoking arm to smoke.

Krumboltz (1966), writing for the school-counselor, refers to counter-conditioning as emotional learning and lists three additional behavioral-counseling techniques:

1. Operant learning or shaping, where desired behaviors are reinforced and attention is given to rewarding successive approximations and later to the ratio of reinforcement to the behavior.

2. Imitative learning, or the use of modeling techniques to train and reinforce new behaviors.

3. Cognitive learning, which involves behavior and grade contracts (as presented in Thompson and Poppen 1972), role-playing (rehearsal of new behaviors), and verbal instructions.

The behavioral counselor's role is to employ reinforcement techniques as counselor and consultant. As a counselor, he uses reinforcement when the student is making honest gains toward achieving the goals he has set for himself. As a consultant, he applies reinforcement principles in working with teachers and parents in restructuring the student's environment in a way that would reinforce adaptive behavior or extinguish maladaptive behavior. (Williams and Anandam [1973] present some effective procedures for doing this, as do Krumboltz and Thoresen [1969].)

## Counseling Goals

The ultimate outcome of behavioral counseling is to teach students to become their own behavior-modification experts; that is, to teach students to program their own reinforcement schedules. It would be even more desirable to encourage students to move from extrinsic to intrinsic reinforcement, which will happen when they are able to derive personal satisfaction from pleasing themselves with their accomplishments regardless of outside recognition. To the above ends, we recommend that all third-grade students be taught the process of behavior modification so that:

1. They will know when it is being done to them.
2. They will be able to become their own behavior-modifiers.
3. They will one day function naturally and genuinely as reinforcing persons.

## GESTALT THERAPY

### Definition

Gestalt therapy, as developed by Perls (1969), focuses on the here-and-now thoughts and feelings people are experiencing. The focus is directed toward the way you are *now* rather than on how you became what you are, why you do what you do, or what you are going to do tomorrow. Gestalt therapy has often been referred to as concentration therapy because, among other objectives, it is aimed at assisting people to increase awareness of their present experience and at frustrating attempts to break out of this awareness. Another aspect of concentration is to move toward developing smoothly emerging and receding figure-ground relationships so that the person can give full attention to the task at hand (figure) while leaving everything else in the background.

Gestalt therapy, as an existential approach, is not directed toward symptom identification and personal analysis, but rather toward total existence and integration. Integration of the fragmented parts of a person's life and maturation (taking responsibility for one's own life) are never-ending processes and are directly related to a person's awareness of the here and now.

A gestalt is initiated as a new need arises. When a need is met, the gestalt it organized becomes complete and no longer exerts an influence on the organism. This enables attention to be directed toward other needs and the corresponding formation of new gestalten. Unfulfilled needs form incomplete gestalten, which clamor for attention and thus block the formation of new gestalten. These unfulfilled needs (incomplete gestalten) are referred to as unfinished business.

### View of Human Nature

From the gestalt point of view, a human being is normal and healthy if he is reacting as a total organism and not as a disorganized or disoriented organism. Gestaltists, believing that many persons tend to fragment their lives, emphasize the development of unity and integration in the normal personality. Gestaltists believe that human beings have the potential to become self-regulating. To accomplish this independence, one must come out of his private world, work for himself, and learn himself. The ultimate purpose of development is for a person to mature, grow up, become aware of his areas of incompleteness, and complete his personality.

Many systems of counseling tend to deal only with the cognitive mode of human functioning while ignoring the emotional and sensory modes of experiencing. "The total organism thinks, not just the brain," is an accurate statement of the gestalt point of view. Perls (1969) wrote "that awareness per se—by and of itself—can be curative." With full awareness a state of organismic self-regulation develops, the total organism takes over, and we can rely on its wisdom. While the focus of gestalt therapy is *not* on collecting symptoms, it does support the idea of listening to your body or paying attention to what your body is trying to tell you about what you are doing. For example, the headache, tic, or rash you develop before undertaking a new task might be helpful in identifying your real feelings about the project.

Perhaps Perls's comment (1969), which has been printed on various posters as the "Gestalt Prayer," best summarizes some of the gestalt views about human nature:

> I do my thing, and you do your thing.
> I am not in this world to live up to your expectations
> And you are not in this world to live up to mine.
> You are you, and I am I,
> And if by chance, we find each other, it's beautiful.
> If not, it can't be helped.

### Method of Counseling

Counseling based on the principles of gestalt therapy remains focused on the here and now, and does not delve into a past that cannot be altered. If past problems are considered, it is important that they be updated to the present as unfinished business. The purpose of counseling is to identify the holes and voids (or unfinished business) in the person's life and to examine how he fills or represses these voids. The main task of counseling is to assist the student in getting past the impasse blocking need-fulfillment and therefore blocking completion of a gestalt.

A helpful way to begin a counseling session is to ask the student to relate his present thoughts and feelings and then to conclude the statement by saying, "I am responsible for that." Besides bringing the student's awareness to the here and now, the statement also focuses on the student's responsibility for directing his own life.

Questions beginning with *why* can only lead to *because* and avoidance of dealing with the fragments and holes in one's life. It is much more useful to speak of *how* and *what*, which confines answers to things that can be changed. Gestaltists believe that neurotics see their survival as depending on their continuing to repress, to censor, and to defeat the therapist's efforts to penetrate their defenses.

Gestalt therapy offers several techniques that are useful to the school-counselor and the teacher. In fact, Janet Lederman's book, *Anger in the Rocking Chair* (1969), is an excellent example of how gestalt techniques can be applied in the classroom. For the counselor, the following methods are suggested in addition to those presented in the chapters on individual and group counseling:

1.  When unfinished business involves another person, the student can be encouraged to complete it by engaging in a dialogue with that person. If the other person is not present, the student can talk to an empty chair and even play his projection of what the other person is saying back to him.
2.  Playing the projection has the value of determining what is really happening with the individual as opposed to what is happening with others. Many times it is easy to avoid an impasse by throwing "personal garbage" on other people.
3.  Most counseling interviews can be improved with *I* language because responsibility for feelings, thoughts, and behavior rests with their rightful owner.
4.  Role-playing reversals are a helpful method for tapping into previously unrecognized feelings. Based on the theory that much behavior represents reversal of latent impulses, the student may be asked to role-play the opposite of the behavior or feeling he or she has been overdoing. For example, the introvert may be asked to role-play an extrovert or a "slave" might be asked to play a "master."
5.  Role-playing the voices of indecision within a person (the voices of topdog and underdog) is helpful for breaking through

impasses where decisions have been avoided. Topdog, representing the voice of Freud's superego, moralizes, condemns, bosses, proclaims *shoulds* and *oughts*, and makes threats. Underdog fights back by rationalizing, making excuses, being passively resistant, and procrastinating.

6. Working with dreams is helpful to the gestalt therapist only if they are used to integrate rather than to interpret. Dream fragments are thought to represent holes, or things missing in our lives. Possibly dream fragments represent the things we avoid. Gestalt therapists ask their clients to act out each fragment of the dream and to let dialogues develop between the fragments in order to integrate the parts into a meaningful whole. By acting out parts of the dream in the first-person singular, real feelings and thoughts are revealed from the voices of such dream fragments as the "unanswered telephone," and the "road winding off into nowhere."

7. Using fantasy games is helpful in creating personal awareness of "what *I* would like to be in relation to what *I* am." A favorite technique is to ask each person in a counseling group to fantasize being a rosebush and then relating what type of rosebush he would like to be: big, beautiful, long-rooted, with other bushes, thorny, do not pick the flowers, and so forth, are samples of what may result from the activity.

### Counseling Goals

The goal of gestalt therapy is to assist people in achieving unification and wholeness in their lives through increased awareness, concentration, and personal responsibility. A subgoal is to assist people in increasing the rate of their healthy expression of aggression. Aggression is defined as everything individuals do to initiate contact with their environment. Aggressive impulses will be misused if they are not expressed appropriately. Healthy aggression is moving toward objects that are necessary for need-satisfaction and, hence, is necessary for closing gestalts or for destroying figures as they form.

## RATIONAL-EMOTIVE THERAPY

### Definition

Rational-emotive therapy, as developed by Albert Ellis (1973), has often been called the *ABC* of psychotherapy. Ellis believes that many systems of psychotherapy are concerned with *A* and *C*, but not with *B*. Rational-emotive therapy is directed toward *B*. In the *ABC* system, *A* refers to the activating event, *B* to the individual's irrational belief system, and *C* to the emotional consequences. In other words, the same events happen to most people (*A*), but the end result (*C*) is quite dissimiliar over the normal range of the population. Therefore, according to Ellis, some intervening variable between *A* and *C* must be having significant effect on *C*. It appears, then, that what people tell themselves about *A* is the cause of emotional disturbance. Rational-emotive therapy leads the client to dispute his irrational beliefs in favor of adopting a more rational set of beliefs; if this is accomplished, the client will experience higher levels of psychological health.

**View of Human Nature**

Rational-emotive therapy is based on the philosophy of Epictetus (b. ca. A.D. 50): "What disturbs men's minds is not events, but their judgments of events." If we can change our irrational thoughts to rational thoughts and tell ourselves sane rather than insane messages, the consequences of activating events will be viewed in a brighter light, which will allow us more freedom to act effectively the next time we find ourselves confronted by the same events. Rational-emotive therapy puts the individual at the center of the universe, responsible for his own actions and feelings. It holds that the individual is able to intervene (and usually does) between environmental input and emotional output, and therefore the individual is viewed as having considerable control over what he thinks, feels, and does.

Rational-emotive therapy emphasizes self-interest. It is better to love one's neighbor, or at least take care not to harm him, not because it is morally right, but out of self-interest. If one loves his neighbor, it is more likely that society will become a better place in which to live. In other words, self-interest demands social interest, and the rational individual, in the process of seeking self-fulfillment, for that reason will be interested in others. Rational-emotive therapy views human beings as naturally helpful and loving to other human beings, provided that they are not caught in the trap of irrational thinking, which leads to self-hate and self-destructive behavior and eventually to hatred of others.

Hersher (1970) writes that rational-emotive therapists believe that human beings are born to think crookedly and therefore have a tendency to be disturbed even before they begin to assimilate some of the nonsense perpetuated by the culture. Hersher also believes that the whole person exceeds the sum total of his parts, and that people have the rational power to integrate their parts and to make and remake their responses to activating events (external stimuli). Ellis believes that some of our illogical ideas may be rooted in biological limitations, but that most of them come from our upbringing—from parents, teachers, peer group, and mass media. In fact, it may be nearly impossible to grow up in our culture without acquiring a large number of illogical assumptions, which, if followed, lead to self-defeating or neurotic behavior patterns. An example of one such illogical assumption is: "It is essential that I be loved or approved by virtually everyone in my community, and if this does not occur I am a worthless slob." A more sane form of the message would be: "It would be nice if everyone in my community loved and approved of me, but it certainly is not essential to my feelings of well-being that everyone do this."

People, allowing themselves to become trapped by irrational thoughts, will probably find themselves feeling intensely angry, inhibited, hostile, defensive, guilty, anxious, ineffective, inert, uncontrolled, and unhappy. Ellis (1973) has condensed fifteen of what he calls his "supreme necessities" into three primary, unprovable, impossible, and irrational dictates that give people trouble:

1. "Because it would be highly preferable if I were outstandingly competent, I absolutely should and must be; it is awful when I am not, and I am therefore a worthless individual."
2. "Because it is highly desirable that others treat me considerately and fairly, they absolutely should and must and they are rotten people who deserve to be utterly damned when they do not."
3. "Because it is preferable that I experience pleasure rather than pain, the world absolutely should arrange this, and life is horrible and I can't bear it when the world doesn't."

Rational-emotive therapy holds that human beings have almost full responsibility for their lives and certainly have choices about whether to be disturbed or not. That is, human beings can choose to restate all of the above insane messages as sane messages and consequently change the way they feel, think, and behave.

## Method of Counseling

Rational-emotive therapy assists people in attacking such illogical thoughts as those listed above. Only through such attacks can the belief system be altered to produce better consequences resulting from environmental input. Rational-emotive therapists use almost anything in their attempts to demonstrate the illogical nature of insane self-verbalizations. Once the irrationality of a statement has been proven, the next task is to help the client replace it with a more sane statement. The role of the school-counselor, using a rational-emotive approach, would be that of a counter-propagandist who directly contradicts the illogical assumptions of the student. The school-counselor could also employ other persuasive methods, including encouragement, reinforcement, and homework.

Rational-emotive therapy also has been successfully adapted for classroom use in helping both elementary-school and secondary-school children to examine the sources of their feelings and their consequent reactions to these feelings. Consider the following sample case:

1. The activating event at point $A$ is the student's failure to recite in class.
2. At point $B$, the belief system, he has the alternative of telling himself one of two possible messages:

|  $B_1$ | OR | $B_2$ |
|---|---|---|
| "This is unfortunate, I don't like it, and I don't want this to happen again." | | "This is absolutely awful. I'm a hopeless dunce; everybody thinks I'm stupid and this is an utter tragedy." |

3. At point $C$ the consequences of $B_1$ or $B_2$ will probably be:

|  $C_1$ | OR | $C_2$ |
|---|---|---|
| "I feel concerned and displeased and I will try to do better next time." | | "I feel extremely depressed and upset over what happened; how will I ever face those kids in my class again?" |
| *Result:* The student will probably recite correctly the next time. | | *Result:* The student will probably do even worse next time he is called upon to recite. |

Consider another example:

1. Point $A$ could be rejection (it often is). One hundred rejected

persons will probably have many different feelings about rejection, ranging from angry or crushed, to relieved or "don't care."

2. Point $B$, with its two responses $B_1$ (sane) and $B_2$ (insane) to the rejection: "I want $X$ and I am getting $X$-$10$!"

$B_1$ "I feel frustrated."              $B_2$ "I should have been able to win that girl."

When we use *should, must,* and *ought* we are in trouble, because the only absolute may be that there are no absolutes. When we say, "It is more than 100 percent unfortunate that I was rejected," or when we say, "She *should* not reject me," we find that it is tough to get evidence for such statements. If "She *should* not reject me" were a valid statement it would be a law and she could not reject you. Where is the evidence to support the statement "She ought to love me"?

Therefore at $B$ you can say:

$B_1$ "Tough."              OR              $B_2$ "I am destroyed."

The way you think, feel, and behave at point $C$ will depend on whether you took the $B_1$ or $B_2$ route. The $B_1$ route will probably lead to a successful relationship in the future; the $B_2$ route to withdrawal or to serious blocking in the establishment of a new relationship.

**Counseling Goals**

The principal counseling goal of rational-emotive therapy, then, is to alter internal verbalizations from irrational to rational statements in order to prevent the perpetuation of emotional disturbance. Albert Ellis was once a psychoanalyst—using conventional psychoanalytic therapy, he claimed to be about 70 percent effective with his patients. Using his own system of rational-emotive therapy, Ellis claims to be about 90 percent effective. Ellis believes that psychoanalytic therapists have not been completely wrong for the past seventy-five years, but that they have been treating secondary causes of emotional disturbance rather than the true primary cause—people's belief systems. No doubt psychoanalytic therapists would argue that they too have been concerned with self-verbalizations—the superego.

## TRANSACTIONAL ANALYSIS

### Definition

Transactional analysis, as developed by Eric Berne (1961, 1964), is a system of psychotherapy that examines the functional quality and quantity of the individual's three ego-states: parent, adult, and child. Transactions between ego-states are analyzed according to whether they are (1) complementary (transaction is addressed to the ego-state that started the stimulus); (2) crossed (transaction is addressed to an ego-state different from the one that started the stimulus); or (3) covert (when people say one thing and mean another). For example:

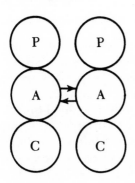         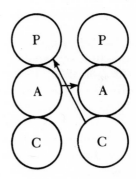

*Complementary Transaction*          *Crossed Transaction*

*Stimulus:* "Did you see today's paper?"

*Response:* "Yes, it's on the kitchen table."

*Stimulus:* "Did you see today's paper?"

*Response:* "Find the paper yourself, no one helps me find things."

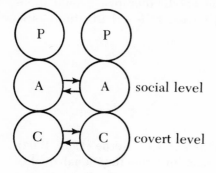

*Covert Transaction*
 *Social level*
 *John:* "Mary, let's study our notes together tonight."
 *Mary:* "Sounds like a good idea to me."
 *Covert level*
 *John:* "Mary, I certainly am attracted to you and would like to become more involved with you."
 *Mary:* "Wow, this is the chance I have been waiting for all quarter!"

According to Berne, people transact to exchange "strokes." A stroke is a unit of social action or recognition of another's presence. An infant is stroked physically, and usually these strokes are accompanied by other messages, either positive or negative. For example, a mother who is caring for her unwanted child may hold him to feed or dress him, but simultaneously she is emitting frustrations and negative feelings, which are received by the child even though he can't understand them. These are crooked or negative strokes, which can become manifest in the adult as "contamination" from the child. Positive strokes may be smiles, verbal praise, or words of acceptance. Negative strokes are seen in frowns, verbal criticisms, and so forth. Young children need many strokes for survival; they absorb whatever they get—positive, negative, or mixed—and they become conditioned to whatever they get.

In addition to ego-states and transactions, the transactional-analysis system also examines rituals, pastimes, games, roles, and rackets. These are defined as follows:

1. Rituals. Simple, stereotyped transactions such as:
   "Hi, how are you?"

"Fine, how are you?"

"Great, good to see you!"

"Let's get together soon!"

2. Pastimes. Relatively safe and superficial talk about non-threatening topics, such as those included in the General Motors' pastime: "I like the gas mileage I get on my new Chevy better than my old Ford."

3. Games. A method of structuring time; played for the purpose of reinforcing opinions about self and others. A game is a recurring series of ulterior transactions complete with a beginning, middle, end, and payoff. Games are devious ways of getting strokes (praise, recognition, attention, appreciation, and affection). For example, the Red Cross game involves rescuing others. If nobody needs rescuing, the Red Cross worker might arrange things so that somebody will.

4. Roles. Played within the game. One game may have as many as five or more roles. When a person plays alcoholic, he may play the *victim*, the *rescuer* when he works for AA, the *connection* when he offers a buddy a drink, the *patsy* when he lends money to a fellow alcoholic for rent, and the *persecutor* when he beats his wife on a drunken binge.

5. Rackets. Pursuing a series of games for the purpose of accumulating points to be cashed in for a future big payoff. The trading stamp analogy applies to the racket activity. People collect trading stamps until they have enough to trade in for a big prize. In life the same thing seems to operate. People collect stamps by running games that appear to make them unwilling victims. When enough stamps are accumulated, the "victim" may try to trade them in for some payoff such as a divorce without alimony.

## View of Human Nature

Transactional-analysis therapists quote Berne as saying that people are born princes and princesses and their parents turn them into frogs. People are viewed as being basically O.K. in the transactional-analysis system. Difficulties arise only when a person has failed to work around some of the bad "scripts" he picked up in childhood from his parents.

Between the ages of three and seven, a child develops a script for his future evolving from accumulated early experiences. He develops his script on the basis of his existential position—that is, the way he feels about himself and others. Berne lists four life positions which are pretty well established by age three. They are:

1. I'm O.K.—You're O.K.
2. I'm not O.K.—You're O.K.
3. I'm not O.K.—You're not O.K.
4. I'm O.K.—You're not O.K.

Berne says that most people are set in their scripts at the "I'm not O.K.—You're O.K." level. At first this seems like a deterministic point of view. But this is where the therapist can intervene and use therapy—both group and individual—to help the individual achieve the adult or "I'm O.K.—You're O.K." position.

According to Berne, the individual person is existential in that he functions in the present and has free-will control of his decisions and actions. Berne parallels the id, superego, and ego of Freud's system with the child (feelings), parent (moral dictates), and adult (conscious control over self). Each person is made up of his earliest feelings—the internal events of his life from birth to five years—which are recorded in the brain as responses to external events. This is the child. The parent is a huge collection of recordings of unquestioned or imposed external events perceived by a person during these same five years. These include the rules, prejudices, and dictates a person hears from his parents and often mistakes for his own unquestioned views. At about ten months of age, the child begins to experience the power of locomotion and gradually finds that he is able to do something growing from his own awareness and original thought. This awareness, analyzing, reacting, and evaluating is the adult aspect of the self. From that time on, according to the factors that shape his life, the individual can react to external stimuli with either of the parts of his self.

Many people believe that the three ego-states are sufficiently complicated so as not to warrant further expansion. However, Berne and others have seen fit to make the model more complex—maybe because human beings are more complex, or maybe because exponents of transactional analysis want to put more distance between Freud and themselves. Some transactional-analysis people protest too much when it is suggested that they have modeled their system after Freud's. In any case, each of the three ego-states has been subdivided into three more PAC-states:

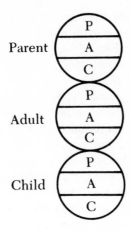

Three types of parents seem to emerge on different occasions: (1) the excluding parent who operates without benefit of his adult or parent; (2) the nuturing parent who provides help; (3) the critical parent who overcontrols and punishes. The parent-state operates like a tape-recorder playing a collection of prerecorded rules for living.

The three adult-types include: (1) the ethically responsible adult; (2) the objective data-processing adult; (3) the personally attractive and responsive adult. The adult state is viewed as a human computer, which stores the data you feed it and retrieves it for the computations it makes. The adult state is said to have no emotions.

The three child-types include: (1) the adapted child—a product of parental training and personal experiences; (2) the little professor —emerging adult in the child; (3) the natural child—untrained infant in the child. The child is the source of our creative, emotional, impulsive, spontaneous, and fun-loving way of being. The child-state feels love and hate, joy and anger, and high and low. The child-state is often seen as the source of people's difficulties; however, in the transactional-analysis system it is the only source for recreation, creativity, procreation, and renewal of life.

## Method of Counseling

One comment frequently made about transactional analysis is that it is more a system of classification and analysis of behavior than a system of psychology. Books on the subject have been and continue to be best-sellers because people are curious about themselves and their comparative states of mental health. In fact, one of the games described by Berne (psychotherapy) involves sitting around and analyzing others' ego-states, rackets, and games. Therefore, most of our summary has considered a description of the system and its concept of the nature of man (Berne 1961, 1964; Harris 1967; James and Jongeward 1971; English 1973).

The counselor's role in transactional analysis is that of a teacher, and the three necessary phases of effective teaching are employed in the presentation of the transactional-analysis system. The first phase involves "tell me about it"; the second, "show me"; and the third, "let me do it." The counselor spends considerable time teaching the terminology and the system and then lets the group try it out. Transactional analysis can be used in one-to-one counseling situations; however, the group-counseling setting offers more fertile ground for transactions and their accompanying analysis. Because each group member learns the system, everyone can counsel as well as be counseled. In addition, since the transactional-analysis system is open to each member, there is no mystery clouding the procedure and expectations of the process and outcome. In fact, each group member will be well enough informed to keep the counselor in line with the correct procedure.

The transactional-analysis process generally starts with each member of the group establishing a contract for what he wants to achieve in the group. These contracts spell out the expectancies of what the individual wants to do, what he wants the counselor to do, and what he would like to have the group do.

Transactional analysis is eclectic in the sense that it employs techniques from other counseling systems to facilitate the gathering of transactional and script data for analysis. One example is the use of fantasies for script analysis. Group members are asked to recall their favorite fairy tale or early childhood story and also the story that they found most upsetting. These stories and their characters are analyzed for possible role or script adoption by the group members as their life-style.

When group members find themselves to be hopeless victims of their life-style, the counselor may grant various individuals permission to "feel what you feel," to "know how you feel," to obtain real strokes, to give real strokes, to live, to enjoy, and to stop hurting oneself. Frequently such procedures may evolve from role-playing activities within the group. Several of the gestalt techniques are also employed in transactional-analysis sessions (James and Jongeward 1971).

## Counseling Goals

The goal of transactional analysis is to bring about behavioral change by freeing the adult from "unhelpful" or self-defeating influences and demands made by the archaic parent and child ego-states. The goal is achieved as long as the person's adult can be hooked into examining his transactions with others. As a tool, transactional analysis can be used to know yourself better; that is, to become aware of how you choose to face your environment. Best of all, transactional analysis provides an opportunity for the individual to become aware of his options. Persons can control the ego-state in which they want to function, rewrite their life's script, and change the way they give and take strokes.

## REFERENCES

Adler, A. 1969. *The Science of Living.* Rev. ed. Garden City, N.Y.: Anchor Books.

Berne, E. 1961. *Transactional Analysis in Psychotherapy.* New York: Grove Press.

————. 1964. *Games People Play.* New York: Grove Press.

Carkhuff, R. 1973. "Human Achievement, Educational Achievement, Career Achievement: Essential Ingredients of Elementary School Guidance." Paper presented at Second Annual National Elementary School Guidance Conference, March 30, 1973, at Louisville, Kentucky.

Dreikurs, R. 1968. *Psychology in the Classroom.* 2nd ed. New York: Harper & Row.

Ellis, A. 1973. "The No Cop-out Therapy." *Psychology Today* 7:56-62.

English, F. 1973. "TA's Disney World." *Psychology Today* 6:45-51, 98.

Eysenck, H. 1964. *Experiments in Behavior Therapy.* Oxford: Pergamon Press.

Frankl, V. 1962. *Man's Search for Meaning: An Introduction to Logotherapy.* Rev. ed. Boston: Beacon Press.

Freud, S. 1949. *An Outline of Psychoanalysis.* Trans. J. Strachey. New York: Norton.

Glasser, W. 1965. *Reality Therapy.* New York: Harper & Row.

————. 1972. *The Identity Society.* New York: Harper & Row.

Harris, T. 1967. *I'm OK–You're OK.* New York: Harper & Row.

Hersher, L. 1970. *Four Psychotherapies.* New York: Appleton-Century-Crofts.

James, M., and Jongeward, D. 1971. *Born to Win.* Menlo Park, Calif.: Addison-Wesley.

Krasner, L., and Ullmann, L. 1965. *Research in Behavior Modification.* New York: Holt, Rinehart & Winston.

Krumboltz, J., ed. 1966. *Revolution in Counseling.* Boston: Houghton-Mifflin.

Krumboltz, J., and Thoresen, C., eds. 1969. *Behavioral Counseling: Cases and Techniques.* New York: Holt, Rinehart, & Winston.

Lederman, J. 1969. *Anger in the Rocking Chair.* New York: McGraw-Hill.

Maslow, A. 1970. *Motivation and Personality.* 2nd ed. New York: Harper & Row.

Perls, F. 1969. *Gestalt Therapy Verbatim.* Lafayette, Calif.: Real People Press.

Rogers, C. 1951. *Client-centered Therapy: Its Current Practice, Implications, and Theory.* Cambridge, Mass.: Riverside Press.

————. 1970. *Carl Rogers on Encounter Groups.* New York: Harper & Row.

Skinner, B. F., and Lindsley, O. 1954. *Studies in Behavior Therapy, Status Reports II and III.* Washington: Office of Naval Research Contract N5 ori-7662.

Thompson, C., and Poppen, W. 1972. *For Those Who Care: Ways of Relating to Youth.* Columbus, Ohio: Charles E. Merrill Co.

Williams, R., and Anandam, K. 1973. *Cooperative Classroom Management.* Columbus, Ohio: Charles E. Merrill Co.

Wolpe, J. 1969. *The Practice of Behavior Therapy.* New York: Pergamon Press.

CHAPTER 3

# Tasks and Techniques of Individual Counseling

What does the school-counselor do in the counseling role? The accompanying table lists some of the major counseling tasks commonly undertaken by school-counselors who use an eclectic theory of counseling. An eclectic approach is based on more than one of the major counseling theories, borrowing techniques from many theories. Most contemporary school-counselors utilize an approach very similar to the one described in this chapter. The table also presents some of the techniques frequently utilized to complete the tasks of counseling.

## LISTENING

The service offered by the school-counselor to those in need of assistance differs from the "man-in-the-street" approach of teachers and administrators. Very little listening occurs during a typical man-in-the-street conversation, because while one party is talking the other party is rehearsing what he intends to say. The school-counselor must avoid this kind of approach. Effective counseling requires that he be an active yet reflective listener to students and teachers who want to tell him about their concerns. To be an active and reflective listener necessitates that the counselor do very little lecturing and that he listen carefully for two important factors, which each student brings to the counseling interview: (1) a problem or area of concern that he has not been able to resolve himself; (2) the feelings he has about what the counselor and the counseling process can do for him.

The school-counselor's first task is to listen for the student's perceptions of his *problem, feelings,* and *expectations* and then to feedback to the student his impression of these three things. Extensive listening, clarifying, and reflecting may be necessary before the student agrees that his counselor sees the problem the way he sees it. Usually students present a number of problems and the school-counselor must help them determine which concern they should try to resolve first. Having agreed on the nature of the problem, the counselor and the student begin to explore the nature of the student's feelings about the problem. The process continues until both agree that the counselor has an accurate picture of the student's feelings. Next, the counselor examines with the student the expectations the student has for counseling. If the student's expectations are in line with the counselor's modus operandi, counseling proceeds to the next phase. If, on the other hand, the student's expectations for counseling are out of the counselor's realm of functioning, the student must know this. The counselor should only offer a service he can adequately perform and should give the student the choice of accepting or rejecting it.

| COUNSELING TASKS | COUNSELING TECHNIQUES |
| --- | --- |
| Listening: Identify the counselee's problem(s), feeling, and expectations | Listening dyad |
| | Sentence completion |
| | Squiggles |
| | Media (video-tape replay) |
| Relating: Analyze the relationship | Descriptive discussion |
| | Inner circle |
| Looking: Determine what is happening | Behavior counting |
| | Shadow |
| | Inventory of the day |
| Evaluating: Allow the counselee to judge his own actions | Empty chair |
| | Imaginary peer group |
| Searching: Specify alternatives | Divergent thinking |
| | Ideal model |
| Predicting: Determine consequences and effects | Visualization |
| | Rehearsal |
| Choosing: Specify the action to be taken | Sharing |
| | Categorizing |
| | Blow-up |
| Practicing: Learn new behaviors | Modeling |
| | Systematic desensitization |
| Encouraging: Promote awareness of potential | Strengths testing |
| | Encouragement inventory |
| Summarizing and Closing: Verify perceptions of the interview | Role reversal |

The counselor, by reflective listening, mirrors the student's world. The process of listening clarifies the client's situation for the student as well as the counselor. Frequently, active listening by a counselor allows the student a chance to discover for himself the flaws in his logic or perception. Active-reflective listening also requires that the counselor reflect the content and feeling aspects of the student's message without sounding like a parrot or a tape-recorder. During the early stages of counseling, the counselor simply helps the student to see where he is regarding his concern. As the student moves through the counseling process he will come to better understand what he wants to accomplish and how he can obtain his goal. The process of helping a student to identify where he "is" or where he is "coming from" requires that the student's feelings first be categorized as pain or pleasure; second, labeled correctly; and third, "mirrored" to the student for validation. After extensive practice, the counselor can respond to students' feelings without sounding patronizing or condescending.

Remaining in tune with the student and his message without interjecting advice or cliches is one way of telling him that you care. *Not* to listen to someone is to show monumental disrespect. *Not listening* is one way teachers, principals, and counselors dehumanize education. Conversely, to humanize education, counselors can help people feel good about themselves simply by letting them experience the importance of being heard.

Although most school-counselors certainly would profess to be experts in listening, one of the concerns of the beginning counselor is how to establish a relationship with a client who may be reticent and nonverbal. With such clients, the counselor will need more than his listening-reflective skill and may find certain other counseling techniques useful. By utilizing various techniques, the counselor is able to evaluate his listening *on the spot*.

The *listening dyad* is a variation of a commonly used group-communication game. The listening-dyad game requires pencil and paper and should be explicitly described ahead of time to the client. The counselor listens to the student for a few minutes, after which he attempts to write in concise form what the student has said. The statement is then read aloud and the student is asked to agree or disagree with the accuracy of the message. The message is then cooperatively edited and revised until agreement is reached about the content of the conversation. One of the benefits of this technique is the increased accuracy of communication. It is not generally useful with highly emotional students, however, and is better used when a client appears to be presenting a typical educational or vocational concern.

Often, in beginning counseling courses, counseling students are asked to interact with an adolescent or a child by playing cooperative games (such as puzzles or crosswords) or competitive games (such as chess or checkers). The experience is intended to help the counseling student develop an understanding of youth through observations in an informal setting. Such contacts between counseling students and youth are frequently very therapeutic and motivational.

Similarly, Winnicott (1968) has developed a technique called *squiggles,* which he uses not only to develop rapport, but also as a means of diagnosis. In doing this with children, Winnicott invites the child to play with paper and pencil. "First I take some of the paper and tear the sheets in half . . . , and then I begin to explain. I say, 'This game that I like playing has no rules. I just take my pencil and go like that, and I . . . do a squiggle blind. I go on with my explanation and say, 'You show me if that looks like anything to you . . .' " (p. 100).

Winnicott is rather directive about the way he introduces the game, even though he allows for other activities during the interview. School-counselors find that the squiggles technique promotes communication and allows the counselor to make observations about the child in a nonthreatening setting. Obviously, the technique is not intended for use by secondary-school counselors but by elementary-school counselors who are attempting to communicate with young children. Winnicott points out that some children want to make the squiggles a "points game" with a winner and loser. Competitive games add extra dimensions to the relationship and increase the possibilities for observation and interaction.

One of the questions asked by school-counselors who engage children and adolescents in competitive games is, "Should I play to win?" Obviously, each counselor must decide for himself about winning or losing. One child psychotherapist plays to win and states, "I don't really think that therapists who fake or hold back in games are ruining anybody, but I do believe they may be overlooking what might be the highest value of the activity—exposure to healthy behavior in the person of the therapist" (Clements 1968, p. 61). Perhaps the only caution for the counselor who plays to win is that it may be necessary to develop new rules and to use handicaps so that the child or adolescent can conceivably win in a fair game.

Another technique to use during the early part of a counseling interview is *sentence completion.* One of the sentence-completion techniques that has proven to be very helpful to elementary-school counselors faced with nonverbal pupils is the *I used to be a____but now I'm a____*game (Padgett 1970). Counselors can use this as a discussion-starter by asking the counselee to fill in the blanks with the names of animals, types of cars, and so forth. Sentence completion has been used by some group counselors to open a discussion of changes in group members, such as "physical changes during my junior high school years." Other techniques such as *ghetto man* and *revolting menus* are fascinating to use with children of all ages (Padgett 1970). Ghetto man consists of describing the life of a person living in the inner city. Revolting menus is a topic that allows nearly everyone to contribute.

Finally, one technique, which may demonstrate the ultimate in listening for some types of students, is the use of audio-tape or video-tape recordings for the counselee's problem presentation. Research using the video-tape recorder as the listener is now being conducted at the University of Tennessee (White 1972). Initial experiences indicate that it may be easier for extremely verbal clients to monologue their concerns to a video-tape recorder than to a counselor. The problem-presentation tape of five or ten minutes' duration becomes the content of the counseling interview. Together, the counselor and the student view the replay and discuss not only the problem but also *how* the concern was presented.

## RELATING

The school-counselor has a responsibility for determining how well he is relating to the students, especially during the early interviews in a counseling relationship. The counselor has available some techniques he can use to determine whether he possesses a positive attitude toward the student he is counseling. One method for determining whether a relationship is potentially positive or negative is to have a brief discussion of the student with another person— someone who will treat the discussion confidentially. After the discussion is completed, the content of the *descriptive discussion* can be rated as highly positive, positive, neutral, negative, or highly negative. If the rating of the descriptive discussion is negative, the school-counselor has the choice of attempting to work through and change his negative impressions of the student, or of referring the student to someone else for counseling.

Thompson's research (1969) indicates that there are students who are not well accepted and in some cases are "unwanted" by

certain school-counselors. It would be idealistic to expect all counselors to relate well to all students. Rather than make such an assumption, the counselor questions the students' "likability" and his own
bias toward certain clients or types of clients. By using techniques
such as the descriptive discussion, the counselor helps himself to
avoid developing stereotyped attitudes toward certain groups of
clients or types of students. The descriptive discussion is also valuable because it enables the counselor to review his actions with the
student and consider plans for further counseling contacts. Using this
technique forces the school-counselor to consider his relationship
with each person in an individual manner. The school-counselor
works to expand his sensitivity to people and increase his acceptance of differences in life-styles. He does this so as to have fewer and
fewer students who rate low on his descriptive discussions.

Another problem frequently encountered by students entering
counseling is the determination of what types of information can be
shared in counseling and how much self-disclosure is expected.
Yalom (1970) has discussed how too much self-disclosure too soon
in counseling is a characteristic of the counseling dropout. Revealing
information about oneself puts a person in a vulnerable position.
How the self-disclosure is received determines whether the relationship becomes more trusting or more fragile. A simple diagram showing an "inner circle" and various levels of social relationship has
been developed by Lazarus (1969) and is suggested as a technique to
be used to answer student questions about self-disclosure. Drawing
an inner circle demonstrates to the student that all people have a private
world and that the counselor will not overpower him or expect him
to tell private thoughts unrelated to the immediate concern. The
counselor draws concentric circles around the private world or inner
circle in order to help the student identify levels of relationship common to all people. The counselor and student can discuss how relationships differ among those next to the inner circle (confidants),
those farther from the inner circle (acquaintances), and those even
farther away (superficial contacts). The counselor lets the student
know that the counseling relationship usually develops similarly to
that with a close acquaintance or a confidant, depending upon the
nature of the problem. In effect, the inner-circle technique helps
clarify the expectations for counseling by illustrating how too little
or too much self-disclosure can impede the process of counseling.

## LOOKING

The second task in the counseling process is to help the student examine what he is presently doing to resolve his conflict. The man-on-the-street approach is used to explore the *whys* behind the student's behavior. Again, as with his listening technique, the counselor uses looking techniques that are somewhat unique. He asks clients to describe their behavior rather than their motives. When asked to discuss *what* he has been doing, the student will probably launch into a series of *why* answers. In fact, the counselor may be the first person to insist that the student respond to the question, "*What* are you doing?"

It is probable that the student has rationalized his behavior to the point that he does not see a need for change. The school-counselor who wants to help the student stop rationalizing and act more responsibly will focus on present behavior. Helping the student put his behavior "on the table" for evaluation is a significant achievement. It is not easy to discuss behavior—especially if what the student has been doing sounds even worse when said aloud. The key step in Glasser's reality-therapy process (1965) may be the act of having the person talk about what he is doing.

Probably one of the most difficult tasks in the counseling process is helping the client ascertain his behaviors and actions. No doubt many students suffer from such distorted focus or disintegrated perceptions that their descriptions of their behaviors are unreliable. Generally, students who are interested in changing a personal habit are unaware of the frequency of their habit—for example, how many fights they have daily. In this case, the counselor may suggest what might be called *behavior counting*. While a wrist counter is used by many behavioral counselors, a mark on a 3 × 5 card is sufficient for most recordings. One ingenious student simply tore the edge of the card to record each occurrence of a certain behavior. Behavior counts can be made of one's own actions or those of another person causing one a problem, such as a parent or teacher. One elementary-school child, who began his counting in order to prove how "ugly" his teacher was to him, tore up his counting card in disgust when he admitted to himself that he, rather than the teacher, was really instigating their conflicts. The act of counting occurrences of the teacher's behavior kept him too busy to bait her, and no fights took place between them.

For some reason, some students are unable to monitor their own behavior, but are quite willing to use the *shadow technique*. The shadow technique requires that the client bring one of his friends with him to the counseling interview. The counselor trains the friend to shadow the student and record his behavior. The shadow's report helps both student and counselor identify what the student actually is doing.

The *inventory of the day* is another technique the counselor can use to help the counselee be more specific and thereby *see* what is happening. The inventory of the day has been used beneficially by Adlerian counselors for a number of years. An accounting of the sequence of the happenings of the day serves to identify unnoticed patterns of behavior or interactions that trigger conflict. Similarly, having the student recall the specific dialogue of a critical incident, such as an argument, can lead to uncovering the antecedents and consequences of certain significant actions.

## EVALUATING

Once the student's behavior is specified or "on the table," the counselor must assist the student in self-evaluation of the behavior. The man-on-the-street approach makes an immediate judgment and tells the student that his behavior is "lousy." The counselor avoids making judgments of the behavior but reacts to the client in such a way as to help him judge. If any change is going to occur, the student has to tell himself that his behavior is "lousy." The counselor should ask the student how his behavior is helping himself or others. If the student admits the behavior is not helpful, the counselor moves to the next step in the counseling process.

The main distinguishing aspect of counseling, which sets it apart from normal communication or conversation, is that the counselor remains nonjudgmental. In fact, being nonjudgmental is probably the one counselor behavior common to all of the many different counseling approaches. At least two techniques can be used to help the student see the contrast between his evaluation of his behavior and an evaluation by someone with a different perspective. By using the *empty-chair* technique, the counselor can add to the counseling interview a third party with a contrasting view, without espousing the opposing viewpoint himself. The empty chair is "occupied" by an imaginary person who is given statements of opinion by either the client or, in some instances, the counselor. If the technique is used properly, the student can develop debate otherwise impossible to experience in real life. The empty-chair technique is usually superior to the often-given advice that students "talk to an adult" in order to get a contrasting opinion. The advice of talking to an adult usually fails because the adults have no desire to have their ideas challenged, let alone to hear the "inane" ideas of youth. Some adults, who seem very reasonable to other adults, may have a nearly insoluble personality conflict with some students.

An *imaginary peer group* can be used to allow the student to have his behavior evaluated by his peers without making his concern public. The student, by projecting what he assumes to be his peers' positions, begins to determine whether his own viewpoint on an issue is a majority or a minority position. Also, he can identify those peers who might assist or block him in any action he may want to take to change his behavior.

Another technique that is sometimes useful at this stage in counseling is to ask the student to *guess* about how his present behavior or misbehavior helps him. What is the goal of the student's behavior? The school-counselor uses his knowledge of Adlerian or individual psychology to help both himself and the student guess from a continuum of four basic goals of behavior. The four goals are attention-getting, revenge-seeking, power-struggling, and inadequacy-displaying. According to the theory of guessing, naming the goal causes the client, even a young child, to place a negative value upon the misbehavior and to almost intuitively move toward a different goal. The guessing is best done with extreme tentativeness. A guess is good only if the student accepts it as having been the goal of his behavior. The counselor is alert to any discrepancy between the client's verbal and nonverbal responses to the guess. Frequently clients, especially children, deny the goal verbally, but accept it by their nonverbal response. The counselor who notices a nonverbal recognition points this out to the student for validation. For example, children who are trying to boss an adult through power-struggling might deny their intentions, while at the same time they smile and look rather proud of the achievements of their misbehavior. Because guessing about goals is so similar to making interpretations about another person, it is best done only when the counseling relationship is firmly established, and even then it should be used infrequently and without insistence.

## SEARCHING

When the student has labeled his behavior as unsatisfactory, the counselor continues the counseling by encouraging the student to search for alternative behaviors that might be helpful. Actually writing the alternatives on paper is a good counseling technique, for it aids the student in searching for appropriate actions. Asking the student, "What could you do that would help you?" is a move toward changing the focus to new behavior. The student who has been engaged in fighting may answer, "Well, I guess I could stop punching Joe." The counselor agrees and says that *stopping* the punching may be helpful; however, he now restates his question: "What are some things you can *start* doing which could help you?" The searching phase of the counseling interview resembles the commonly used group activity of brainstorming. No evaluating of the student's alternative plans of action is allowed at this time since evaluating alternatives during the searching phase tends to block creativity. The counselor wants the student to think freely about alternatives without fear of negative criticism.

The counseling task of searching for alternative ways of behaving requires divergent thinking by both the student and the counselor. Perhaps the most effective techniques to use at this point are variations of Guilford's *divergent-thinking* tasks (1968). By knowing the concept of divergent-thinking skills, the client learns to search for alternatives. For example, the counselor might ask the student to list as many problems as he can which are caused by some common object, such as an outdated telephone book. The process of listing a variety of problems caused by some object will help the student understand the kind of thinking required at this stage in counseling, which may unblock his thinking and make him a more creative and effective brainstormer. The counselor is free to participate actively in the divergent thinking in order to demonstrate dramatic and creative alternatives to the student's problem. Naturally, the increased brainstorming skills of the client should serve to generate viable solutions to his problems.

To identify and discuss an *ideal model* can also uncover unique alternatives. The student identifies someone he knows who can do what he wants to be able to do. A specific person should be named, and how the ideal model actually behaves should be stated. Using the ideal-model technique to search for alternatives is somewhat different from selecting a model to emulate for skill development. Clients are more likely to develop skills or take suggestions from models not too unlike themselves; however, descriptions of ideal models lead to the generation of more creative alternatives for people who are trying to solve problems. The basic idea of searching for alternatives is to list as many ideas as possible rather than stopping at two or three which appear to be immediate problem solutions. Once the student's list is completed, the counselor moves to the next phase in the counseling process.

## PREDICTING

The counselor's next task is to assist the student to learn to predict possible outcomes of the alternatives. The counselor does this in a number of ways. For example, he may ask the student to role-play himself in one of the alternative behaviors or roles. Questions such as "How do you see this helping you?" frequently help the student to sort out viable plans of action. The counselor may even focus on the empathy the student has for the others involved by asking, "How would your friends [or family] be affected by this plan?"

The essential question for this counseling task is, "How do you see a specific action helping you?" A closely related question, which can assist the counselee in making a prediction, is, "Can you see yourself doing that action?" *Visualization* can be used to make this question more concrete and vivid by having the student project himself into a situation in which he enacts one of his alternatives. During the visualization, seemingly logical alternatives for the student often do not "fit" because negative emotional reactions are evoked. The visualization can also help to identify a plan that seems to be a very natural and comfortable thing for him to do.

Any *role-playing* done at this stage in counseling is better made very concrete and can be perfected by adding the techniques of *rehearsal* and *negative rehearsal*. Sports teams usually "walk through" their new plays and then gradually accelerate the process until they finally perform at full speed. The walk-through or rehearsal process has advantages similar to those of visualization. Additionally, rehearsals may be used to assist in the processes of choosing and encouraging because the extreme concreteness of the rehearsal helps the client sort out the top-priority alternative from his second priority —thus his choice becomes more obvious. The practice obtained in realistic rehearsals encourages the student because he gains confidence and usually has a more successful implementation of his selected alternative. One student, in counseling with one of the authors, was so specific about her rehearsed confrontation with her father about an issue that she actually planned to meet him in the hallway between the dining room and the kitchen. With such specificity, it was not surprising that her plan was carried out almost exactly as it was rehearsed; and she had her first real discussion with her father in over two years.

During the use of the negative-rehearsal technique, the client and the counselor try to determine the one thing the client should avoid doing, which might defeat him in his plan. For example, a student who has had a conflict with a teacher might decide that it would be unwise to mention a teacher's previous "mistake." First, the teacher might not agree that she was mistaken; second, referring to the old mistake would be much like reopening an old wound. In the safe confines of the counselor's office, the client can actually rehearse the mistakes he hopes to avoid in his contacts with the teacher. Doing the negative rehearsal should help the student determine whether he can avoid these expressions around the teacher; if so, he can predict some success for the plan.

## CHOOSING

One of the most humanistic acts a counselor, teacher, or parent can perform is to allow young people to choose. Allowing someone to choose communicates: (1) I care enough about you to consider your wishes and preferences, and (2) I believe you have the ability to make helpful choices. The school-counselor assigns the student to practice for a specified time, both during and outside of the counseling interview, one or more of his alternative behaviors. Practicing new behavior between counseling contacts becomes homework for clients who are trying to develop new modes of behavior. In counseling, homework assignments help the student learn to develop commitment for changing his behavior.

Heath (1964) has written that lack of commitment is a frequent and difficult-to-overcome developmental block. Generally, it is wise to obtain a written commitment from the student describing the homework he will do before seeing the counselor again. The next interview should begin by having the student report about his plan. If the contract was not kept, it can be discarded; a new one should be written and signed. Responding to unattempted or incompleted homework merits some further comment. There are three things the counselor wants to avoid doing: (1) the counselor does not want to ridicule the student for failing to do what was planned; (2) the counselor does not manipulate the student with an "I thought you would do it for me," response; (3) the counselor avoids excusing the student by statements, such as "I didn't really think you could do it." In other words, the counselor avoids making judgments about the incomplete homework. The counselor resists blaming, excusing, or pressuring the student; rather, the counselor responds by asking the student whether he is still interested in trying to solve his problem and whether he intends to do the homework in the future. Either a new plan is developed or a recommitment to the former plan is obtained. In essence, what the counselor does is to "recycle" the student through the counseling process, allowing the student to make his own judgments about his behavior and plans. Seldom will the counselor have to rewrite a contract with a student more than twice. A typical counseling-homework assignment might be scheduling a conference with a teacher to work out a personal conflict by making an effective complaint (Thompson and Poppen 1972; Weinberg 1969).

During the task of having the client choose a priority alternative, the counselor may be very active. If the counselor has used some of the suggested techniques during the preceding tasks, the counselor and student should have developed a relationship which allows them to challenge and dispute each other's ideas. The stronger the relationship, the more the counselor is able to *share* his thoughts and feelings in a way that benefits the student. What the school-counselor really hopes to do is to share his reactions and feelings during the counseling interview in a way that enriches the student's experience. Sharing was once considered taboo for the school-counselor but becomes appropriate when the counselor understands why it is dangerous to share his ideas and feelings too early in counseling (Gendlin 1970). The danger, of course, is that the student may accept the counselor's feelings and thoughts as his own without challenging or modifying them to suit his own personality. The *sharing* technique, properly utilized at the appropriate time in the counseling relationship, can provide the client with additional perspective before he chooses a course of action.

One idea the counselor and student might share is whether the proposed courses of action are tentative or irrevocable. This type of sharing allows the counselee to rate the risk-taking required by each alternative. Naturally, plans having irrevocable consequences involve higher-risk factors.

*Blow-up*, credited to Ellis (1971), is another technique the counselor might use to assist the student in seeing possible consequences and, thereby, making a better choice. One school-counselor reports using blow-up outside of a counseling interview with a principal who was facing a rather crucial parent-teacher meeting. The consequences of an ineffective meeting seemed dire to the principal until he considered what might be the worst thing that could happen if the meeting went badly. Would he be fired? "Unlikely," he thought, "because I have tenure." Would he lose the support of his staff or the parents? "Unlikely, because very few people would feel I am responsible for the development of the problem or for its resolution." After developing a more honest assessment of the value of the meeting to himself personally and professionally, the principal entered the meeting, performed admirably, and actually helped resolve the conflict.

## PRACTICING

After a choice of a plan of action has been made by the student, the school-counselor often has the task of helping him practice and learn new behaviors. Frequently, some of the practicing occurs within the counseling interview. Students who have similar concerns, and who are at various levels of development in learning a new behavior, may practice together in groups. Many times the counseling process consists of practicing a new skill in the interview or doing homework on the skill between counseling interviews. The subsequent counseling interview may consist of evaluating the homework and completing additional practice.

During this phase of counseling the counselor functions very much like a good teacher. There are a number of techniques for helping the student to practice a new behavior. Some of the techniques have already been discussed. For example, role-playing, visualizing, rehearsing, and negative rehearsing are effective means of learning. Sometimes the counselor uses more specific techniques for more specific concerns. An example would be the use of systematic desensitization procedures for students who suffer from some type of anxiety, such as a test anxiety (Weinstein 1969). The counselor needs special training in order to develop the skill to use relaxation and desensitization techniques.

Learning by "modeling" through live demonstrations, video-tape recordings, or audio-recordings is another strategy for the counselor to use in helping students practice new behaviors. Some of the most creative practicing techniques are combinations of some of these techniques. One example is the combining of role-playing with video-tape modeling. In some instances, students are able to role-play their reaction in a specific situation, play it back on the video-tape recorder, evaluate the inappropriate behaviors in the role-playing, and correct the behaviors in a new role-playing situation.

## ENCOURAGING

When, if ever, would a school-counselor use encouragement or reinforcement during counseling? The argument *against* using either is that such counselor behavior might limit the student's freedom to make his own choices and decisions. In fact, reinforcement counseling is frequently rebuked as dehumanizing, in that students may be manipulated rather than receive the benefits of an I-thou, person-to-person, relationship. Peters (1970) makes a distinction between encouragement and reinforcement. He views encouragement as increasing confidence and motivation; reinforcement, on the other hand, is limited to producing specific behavioral changes.

The argument *for* using reinforcement is that counselors cannot avoid being positive or negative during counseling interviews—because of this, it is better for counselors to be aware of their reinforcement behavior and to do it systematically rather than haphazardly.

Another point of view, which ameliorates some of the conflict between the pro and con arguments, asks what is wrong with encouraging or positively reinforcing students when they are making progress toward meeting counseling goals that they have established for themselves. One example might be when the counselor participates in the practicing activities described above. The counselor might systematically reinforce any appropriate behaviors exhibited during role-playing or rehearsing activities in order to help students learn new behaviors more efficiently. Most people probably recall how a significant someone gave them the encouragement needed to take the next big step at some stage of their development.

One definition of learning might be the discovery that something is possible. The task of choosing a plan of action is of little value unless the student has the courage to act. Encouragement can be obtained by utilizing *strengths testing* either within the interview or as a homework assignment. If it is done within the interview, the counselor and the student both list what they consider to be the student's major strengths. The listings should be as clear as possible and in behavioral terms. Rather than stating that a person is "the life of the party," statements should be made about how someone enlivens a party, such as, "good at telling funny jokes," or "can get a group singing." The strengths test is intended to show the student that he *does* complete constructive acts. Encouragement is more than having the student *feel* important and worthwhile; it *shows* him that he has the potential to *do* important and worthwhile things.

Another activity that might be used during this phase of counseling is to have the student list all the sources of encouragement that exist in his life. Completing the inventory helps his self-confidence. During the period when a student is trying to change a behavior or enact an improvement plan, it may be important for him to increase his association with the sources of encouragement.

## SUMMARIZING AND CLOSING

The counseling interview should close by having the student summarize the main points of the counseling. In addition to providing a quick review, the student's summary will emphasize those things significant to him, thereby allowing the counselor to evaluate his own perceptions of the counseling. In fact, counselors might well employ the technique of asking the student to summarize the interview content whenever the counseling session is at an impasse. A review of the interview content usually helps to identify the impasse so that more fruitful dialogue can continue.

During the counseling task of ending the interview, it is important to verify perceptions of what happened during the interview. Another specific way to close the interview is to have the counselor use *role reversal*. To reverse roles the counselor and client might actually switch chairs. Each of them then role-plays the other person for a few minutes, reviewing the most important aspects of the counseling interview. One advantage of role reversal is that it allows the counselor to evaluate whether he is being understood, whether he is allowing the student to make choices, and whether he is accurately sharing his thoughts and feelings with the student.

At the close of each interview, the student decides whether to make an appointment for another interview or to terminate the counseling. Of course, the school-counselor will not try to force anyone to participate in the counseling process. While the scheduling of appointments may be helpful for some students, the school-counselor will operate with enough flexibility to keep an open-door policy. In fact, the counselor's open-door policy should include time to meet with students in places other than his office, since the office setting itself may be a barrier to establishing helpful counseling contacts.

## THE NEED FOR RESPECT AND TRUST

This chapter presents what might be termed an eclectic approach to counseling. In contemporary school counseling, techniques from several different counseling systems seem to have utility. The school-counselor has the task of identifying what works best for him in assisting students to become independent.

The preceding sections of this chapter have suggested techniques that can be used during the counseling interview to enrich the counseling process. We caution that proper timing is essential. Suggestions have been made as to the approximate stage in counseling when each technique would be most appropriate. Another caution: Counseling is more than completing a number of activities in sequence—it must be based upon honest care and involvement on the part of the counselor. Techniques will not cover a lack of basic acceptance and mutual respect.

Of course, nothing works for the counselor who has failed to establish a comfortable counseling relationship free of mistrust and disrespect. How, then, does a counselor build trust? Trust exists in relationships where people feel wanted and worthy. Trust also exists between two persons who allow for each other's mistakes. Real trust between two persons survives ventilation of hostilities and feelings of hate, anger, hurt, and resentment.

How can mutual respect be established between counselor and student? The counselor can become a "mutual-respect" model by not infringing on the rights of the student and by giving him full attention. The price for obtaining mutual respect does *not* include the abolishment of limits. Frequently, the student needs to know that the counselor cares enough to set limits, that he cares enough to say *stop* or *no*. Just as frequently, though, the student needs to know that the counselor cares enough to see that students are granted rights and freedoms appropriate for their age. In a relationship based upon mutual respect, limits and freedoms coexist. The active and helpful school-counselor demonstrates that he understands the role of limits and rights in mutual-respect relationships by exhibiting them both in counseling and as a person in noncounseling settings.

## REFERENCES

Clements, J. 1968. "The Game Is the Thing" *Voices* 4:60-64.
Ellis, A. 1971. "Debate: Albert Ellis vs. Daniel Casriel—On Anger." *Rational Living* 6:2-21.

Gendlin, E. 1970. "A Short Summary and Some Long Predictions." In *New Directions in Client-Centered Therapy*, ed. J. Hart and T. Tomlinson. New York: Houghton-Mifflin.

Glasser, W. 1965. *Reality Therapy*. New York: Harper & Row.

Guilford, J. P. 1968. *Intelligence, Creativity and Their Educational Implications*. San Diego: Robert R. Knapp.

Heath, R. 1964. *The Reasonable Adventurer*. Pittsburgh: University of Pittsburgh Press.

Lazarus, A. 1969. "The Inner Circle Strategy: Identifying Crucial Problems." In *Behavioral Counseling: Cases and Techniques*, ed. J. Krumboltz and C. Thoresen. New York: Holt, Rinehart & Winston.

Padgett, R. 1970. "I Used to Be a _____, But Now I'm a _____." *Teachers and Writers Collaborative* 3:32-33.

Peters, H. 1970. *The Guidance Process*. Itasca, Ill.: Peacock Publishers.

Thompson, C. 1969. "The Secondary School Counselor's Ideal Client." *Journal of Counseling Psychology* 16:69-74.

Thompson, C., and Poppen, W. 1972. *For Those Who Care: Ways of Relating to Youth*. Columbus: Charles E. Merrill.

Weinberg, G. 1969. *The Action Approach*. Cleveland: World.

Weinstein, F. 1969. "Reducing Test Anxiety." In *Behavioral Counseling: Cases and Techniques*, ed. J. Krumboltz and C. Thoresen. New York: Holt, Rinehart & Winston.

Welch, R. 1971. "A Weight Loss Program for Overweight Adolescent Girls and Its Effects on Self-Concepts." Unpublished dissertation, University of Tennessee, Knoxville.

White, P. 1972. "The Effects of a Specified Videotape Technique on Client Verbal Behavior." Unpublished dissertation, University of Tennessee, Knoxville.

Winnicott, D. 1968. "The Squiggle Game." *Voices* 4:98-112.

Yalom, I. 1970. *The Theory and Practice of Group Psychotherapy*. New York: Basic Books.

CHAPTER 4

# Group Counseling

In *Future Shock* (1970), Toffler points out that man can expect to find it increasingly more difficult to adjust as he moves from one stage of development to the next—that he will experience a form of culture shock as he moves to each new life-stage. Toffler advocates the establishment of groups for the purpose of easing the transitions between stages. For example, temporary groups might help new-comers become acquainted with the services offered in a new community. Certainly transition groups could be used to advantage in the school setting. The counselor, through group work, can assist students in their transition from elementary school into junior high, and through high school and college. Action-oriented groups seem to offer the greatest potential for the counselor helping students within the schools. Many of the principles of individual counseling apply equally well to the conduct of group meetings. Once again the outcome emphasis is on personal-behavior change. Three group-counseling models (8-12 students) and two classroom-group models (20-35 students) are presented for consideration.

## COMMON-PROBLEM GROUPS

As may be implied from its name, the common-problem group (Blocher 1966) focuses on a concern shared by all the group members. Typical common problems are drug abuse, parents, passing grades, dating behavior, sexual problems, and birth control. The common-problem group has the advantage of providing an empathic group setting for the sharing and resolving of deep personal concerns. A frequently heard comment from common-problem group members is, "It is just good to know I'm not the only one who has this problem," which is more than merely a case of misery loves company. Yalom (1970), in one of his studies of group therapy, found a

81

factor of universality, or a feeling of "We're all in the same boat," to be one of the more frequently reported curative factors. Common-problem group members seem to be more open to each other, and trust seems to be established rather easily. One disadvantage of the common-problem group may be the lack of successful models in the group. Often, it is helpful to include in the group some persons who have mastered the problem area or who can serve as "ideal" group members to be modeled by others. Some group leaders have successfully used such individuals as "plants" who demonstrate how the group members should behave.

One of the real problems of getting groups started in the school is the counselor's lack of experience in leading a group. Although he may have been a group member or have had a practicum in individual counseling, hesitancy may exist because of inexperience as a group leader. Lack of experience in leading groups is especially true for many of the older counselors, who were trained prior to the late 1960s. Even now, few counselor-education programs offer a group practicum, while practicums in individual counseling are typical. The counselor can often use highly structured or programmed group activities to ease this situation. The College Entrance Examination Board has developed a series of workbook games in the areas of value-clarification, information-gathering, and decision-making strategies. The activities, called *Deciding*, are designed primarily for junior high school youth, but new materials are being developed for other age-levels. The program is designed so that it might cover a few hours or an entire semester.

*Deciding* relies heavily on some of the value-clarification techniques developed by Raths, Harmin, and Simon (1969). Specific techniques, such as "Twenty Things I Like to Do," "I am Proud," and "Coat of Arms," are taken directly from the work of Simon (1972). The overriding benefit of the materials for the common-problems group is that they do more than help the group members with specific problems; rather, they teach a process of solving problems and making choices.


## CASE-CENTERED GROUPS

The case-centered group, sometimes called C-group (Foreman, Poppen, and Frost 1967) offers the opportunity for each person to counsel as well as to be counseled. Group members bring different concerns to the group. Usually these concerns are relationship problems. For example, teachers or parents might form a group and each member might bring a description of one of her "problem children" to the group as her case. During each meeting, the group focuses on one member's concern until each member has had this opportunity. Case-centered groups offer the advantage of providing group members who may already have worked through another member's problem; consequently, modeling and peer-teaching benefits are additional advantages.

Both common-problem and case-centered groups utilize a problem-solving approach employing many of the following steps:

1. Identify a problem of one of the group members.
2. Describe what has been and what is being done to solve the problem.
3. Evaluate present and past problem-solving behaviors (include inner feelings as a clue to the effectiveness of the behavior or life-style pattern).
4. Brainstorm for alternative behaviors (do not evaluate proposed new behaviors).
5. Predict outcomes of proposed alternative behaviors.
6. Attempt one new behavior (include a group rehearsal of new behavior before trying it outside the group).
7. Report outcome to the group.
8. Recycle the process if necessary.

The case-centered group frequently focuses upon a relationship problem one of the group members is having with someone outside the group. *Relationship analysis* is an extremely productive technique for assessing what is happening in a relationship and deciding what action can be taken for improvement. The characteristics of a balanced or mutually respectful relationship were developed by Missildine (1963). These characteristics are as follows: (1) every relationship should have some *limits* and some definite areas of *freedom;* (2) every person, even a child, should have designated *responsibilities;* (3) *personal recreation* or "time alone" is important. These principles can easily be taught to group members, who then can apply the ideas during the meetings.

The ideas presented here are outlined more fully in *For Those Who Care: Ways of Relating to Youth* (Thompson and Poppen 1972). Essentially, the procedure requires that: (1) the relationship be described; (2) the limits imposed in the relationship be specified; (3) the responsibilities of each member of the relationship be stated;

(4) the degree of freedom within the relationship be noted; and (5) the amount of recreation for each member of the relationship be designated. After these points have been shared with the group, the members can determine whether the relationship is unbalanced and how it needs to be changed in order to regain mutual respect.

## HUMAN-POTENTIAL GROUPS

Human-potential groups (Otto 1967) focus on the group members' personal strengths and positive traits. In human-potential groups the members examine the resources each one has for overcoming blocks to further growth and development. The group restricts itself to criticizing only those things a person can change; seldom do group members criticize more than one behavior at a time.

Strengths-testing exercises are employed to assist individuals in making realistic appraisals of their unrealized potential. A group member may be asked to survey significant people outside the group for their assessments of his strong points. After listing the strengths, the "outside" persons then list one block that may be keeping the member from developing his potential. The exercise becomes more than a sugar-coated ego booster if the raters list specific strengths and are equally specific in explaining the reasons for the choices.

Human-potential groups are directed toward increasing group members' self-worth. One of the best means to focus on self-concept is to examine how to destroy a person's positive self-image. One way to do this is to have the school-counselor interview a student before the group in such a way as to cover the person's strengths. After the short interview, the counselor remarks, "It sounds to me as though you are quite *likable* and capable." If the student agrees, the counselor hands the student a paper sign with the letters *IALAC* ("I am likable and capable"). The other members of the group are then asked to make remarks about the student that tend to destroy a positive self-concept. After each remark, the student tears off a portion of the *IALAC* sign to represent the degree of self-concept destroyed by the remark. The remarks may range from, "This is the fifth time I've called you; get up or you will miss the bus!" to "Won't you ever learn that you need to get eight hours of sleep? I don't know what is going to become of you!"

The group continues to make such remarks until the *IALAC* sign is destroyed. Discussion should center on the reality of the demonstration and include a follow-up exercise in which group members record all destructive remarks heard and made between group meetings. Other human-potential group exercises could focus on active listening, sensory awareness, empathy building, and general training in assertive behavior.

There are numerous resources describing procedures for developing awareness or potential. One example is the Institute for Personal Effectiveness in Children, San Diego, California, which trains teachers in a human-development program. The program utilizes magic-circle sessions and presents activities appropriate for students in elementary schools. Hopefully, it will not be long before adults accept human-potential group activities as a legitimate part of education. Until then, it is unlikely that the public will approve of a school-counselor sitting in a dark room with a group of high school students seated in a circle and fantasizing being a rose. Such sensitivity games are just too "far out" for traditionalists who have never experienced them. In the meantime, there are many valuable activities that can be done while remaining in chairs with the lights on. Some excellent sources describing more practical group activities have recently become available for the counselor's use in school settings. In fact, some of them are directed to classroom teachers (Von Hilsheimer 1970; Hunter 1972).

A number of techniques are common to the various human-potential group programs available for use in school settings. One technique, which increases the interaction and interest in *any* group activity, is the use of *time-out* partners. During any group activity the group leader can call a time-out. Partners meet together for a short time to counsel or coach one another about their group performance or about any strategy each is using. Depending upon the type of group, a number of procedures can be used to select partners. In an ongoing group game, each member picks someone he feels would be most able to listen to him or to assist him in making decisions. At other times, in other games, the member picks someone very unlike himself, and thus learns entirely new perspectives about the game being played. The time-out technique obviously has one other advantage: it prevents the group members from being non-participants or spectators in the group activity by forcing them to talk to another person about what is happening.

## CLASSROOM MEETINGS

Classroom meetings or just plain rap groups are good vehicles for humanizing and improving education. Conducting these meetings and training teachers to conduct them with their students is one of the primary functions of a school-counselor, especially the elementary-school counselor. Glasser (1969) suggests three types of classroom meetings: social-problem-solving meetings, open-ended meetings, and educational-diagnostic meetings.

Classroom group meetings are certainly not a new idea. The Adlerian psychologists have been advocating "democratic discussion" in the classrooms for a number of years. The technique, used by Adlerians, of interviewing the parents of problem children in front of an audience, is strikingly similar to the process advocated by Glasser in the social-problem-solving meeting. Glasser has developed a specific technique of questioning, which is extremely useful in promoting the use of three different types of classroom-group meetings among teachers and school-counselors.

*Social-problem-solving* class meetings concern problems of the class as a group and of any member of the class. Typical problems include truancy, classroom behavior, and home problems. The leader's job in the classroom meeting is to avoid being punitive and judgmental. The classroom meeting provides the opportunity for each group member to judge his own behavior. The discussion is directed toward solving the problem; the solution should never include punishment or fault-finding. One of the rules of the classroom-group meetings is that the group should be seated in a circle (everyone has a front-row seat). No member is allowed to monopolize the meetings or attack any other member unfairly. Also, the students are encouraged to talk one at a time and to speak about their real concerns.

The social-problem-solving meeting in the classroom should be used only when specific personal or group problems arise. Consequently, it is used less frequently than the open-ended or educational-diagnostic type of meetings. One technique that can be used to supplement the social-problem-solving meeting is *effective complaining.* Effective complaining is based upon the assumption that an important skill in solving interpersonal or social problems is to let other people know when you feel abused. The rules of complaining are modifications of those developed by Weinberg (1969). Some of the rules for actually making a complaint, which the group members learn and then attempt to apply in their own lives, are the following:

1. Complain to whoever is infringing on your rights and to no one else.
2. Make only one complaint at a time.
3. Do not ask a person why he is doing something; ask only that he stop.

4. Object only to what can be changed.
5. Rehearse the complaint before making it.

School-counselors and teachers who want to try the game would benefit from reading *For Those Who Care* (Thompson and Poppen 1972). The effective-complaining technique can be used with children in the intermediate grades or with adults. Children quickly become very skilled at complaining in a *helpful* way to classmates, teachers, and friends. When a majority of the students in the school begin to check each other's complaining behavior, overall communication is improved and fewer personal-social problems develop. Effective complaining becomes one strategy to use in resolving interpersonal conflicts. The technique of making good complaints becomes known to all group members and provides a common basis for interaction during the social-problem-solving meetings.

The social-problem-solving meeting can be extremely effective in changing behaviors. Although many advocate its use for changes in self-concept, research indicates it is more valuable for changing behaviors. Welch (1971), using the process with overweight adolescent females, found significant weight loss but insignificant self-concept change.

Open-ended classroom meetings, described by Glasser as being the cornerstone of relevant education, should be used most often—perhaps as frequently as 70 to 90 percent of the time. During the open-ended meetings students are given the privilege of discussing any thought-provoking questions related to their lives. More often than not, student questions will be related to the class curriculum. The uniqueness of the open-ended discussion is related to the fact that, for once, the counselor or teacher is not looking for specific, factual answers.

Generally, open-ended discussions generate thinking that demands analysis, synthesis (creativity), and evaluation skills. Open-ended discussions can begin with the leader posing the question, "What is interesting to you?" One second-grade class went from a discussion about eyes and what people see with their eyes to what it might be like not to see; and, finally, to a blind person's method of reading. The group leader made the discussion as concrete as possible by having the students experience the limitations and feelings a person might have if blind. For example, when the discussion became blocked, the teacher conducted an experiment to determine whether a child whose eyes were shut could identify a quarter in one hand and a dollar-bill in the other hand.

Open-ended discussion topics examine outcomes to *what if* situations found on many tests of creativity. For example, *what would happen if* . . .

1. all people were born the same color or were born green?
2. all but the highest mountains were covered, with water?
3. all the group members had plenty of money and did not have to go to school or work?
4. people everywhere refused to fight in wars even though their leaders ordered them to fight?

The open-ended discussion is more related to promoting changes in thinking than changes in behavior. Glasser (1969) has rather specific suggestions about conducting an open-ended meeting. Counselors and teachers who have implemented open-ended discussions in classrooms have found at least four techniques helpful in getting the discussions started and keeping them constructive.

One of the difficulties in conducting open-ended discussions is how to determine who should be talking and what the group should be talking about. One technique, which is helpful in decreasing the confusion of everyone talking at the same time, is the *focus* game (Sax and Hollander 1972), in which an object is designated the focus and used as though it were a microphone. In other words, one person at a time has the focus, or imaginary microphone. The person with the focus talks about his thoughts on the agreed-upon topic. Other group members may question the person with the focus, but they should not state their opinions until they have it. One teacher, with an extremely verbose and unruly class of disadvantaged students, used a simple hand-mirror as the focus and claimed it resulted in the best discussions she had ever held with that class.

Another technique, which has proven very helpful with unruly students, is *self-monitoring*. Often a school-counselor assumes that students know appropriate group behavior. Many times, with groups of students referred to the counselor because they are behavior problems, the students simply do not know what behavior is expected or how to exhibit the appropriate behavior.

Self-monitoring is a plan for using behavior-modification techniques in group counseling to teach children appropriate group behavior. Each student was given a self-recording sheet containing boxes in which to mark his own behaviors. The plan was as follows:

1. Discuss a topic for five minutes. Every sixty seconds, each student records his behavior. Reward behavior as shown on his

sheet with M & M candy and allow one or two minutes for eating the candy.

2. Present new topic. Follow the procedure described above. Total time: seven minutes.

3. Present a third topic (let students choose topic). Follow the same procedure described above.

The group might begin by talking about "what you do for fun at home." The school-counselor can randomly call "check," usually at intervals of thirty or sixty seconds. If the group members are following the rules they are to give themselves a check. After the discussion is over the group members count their checks and receive one M & M for each check. Sometimes the counselor might give one of the group members a stopwatch and have him function as a timer. Usually, enacting the self-monitoring technique will help group members quickly learn group behavior and the plan can be easily reactivated if group behavior deteriorates.

There are two other techniques that counselors and teachers have found extremely helpful in maintaining an interest in open-ended discussions. One is to ask students to *describe a picture*, another is to have students *finish a story*. In effect, the pictures or stories become the topic of discussion. The idea behind each of these techniques is to get the students to express and share their thoughts. The emphasis is not upon how students feel, but rather upon what they think. Once the students get the idea of the picture game, they can begin bringing their own pictures to the group for discussion. If the counselor has a media center available, pictures can be enlarged and mounted or transposed on an overlay for easy viewing by all group members.

Pictures are hard to find; however, motion pictures intended to promote open discussion about controversial topics are becoming more readily available. A counselor with extensive experience in open-ended classroom meetings made the following comments about using pictures or enrichment materials: "Why not construct a folder for each student? Each time a meeting is held the students could be responsible for bringing a statement of something that is important to him." The student could collect magazine editorials, letters to the editor, song lyrics, advertisements, or cartoons for his folder for use in open-ended meetings.

*Educational-diagnostic* classroom meetings are directly related to topics the class is studying and are used to determine what students know about a subject or what they have learned from studying. The group leader will do this by asking for definitions of terms and elaboration of ideas presented. Another purpose of educational-diagnostic discussion is to examine the depth of the students' learning. Thus, the counselor will utilize *why* questions in order to determine if there has been more than mere memory-level learning. An effective group-discussion leader should withhold his own value judgments. Because the purpose of the educational-diagnostic meeting is to find out what the students know and really understand, the students must feel free to express their thoughts without fear of ridicule or low grades. Classroom meetings are not for grading! In one high school educational-diagnostic classroom meeting, the class went from "What is a fuel shortage?" to "Does it exist?" to "Does a possible fuel shortage pertain to you?" to "What might you do to influence fuel consumers and government officials to conserve fuel?" Other teachers have utilized the discussion format to improve the classroom learning situation by asking the class, "What would you do if you were the teacher?" Students enjoy being teacher when they can experiment with their own ideas. The discussion topic becomes even more relevant if the teacher is willing to allow the students to implement some of their ideas.

While the educational-diagnostic meeting can be good procedure for both students and teacher to use in evaluating learning, there are other methods. Better than continual educational-diagnostic discussions is the *cooperation* game, which involves students interacting with each other and with materials in a way that demonstrates their understanding of a concept or topic.

Materials necessary for the cooperation game include a large sheet of poster-board, a tube of paste or glue, a box of colors, a pair of scissors, and six or eight magazines for each subgroup of students. The class group should be divided into small subgroups. Each subgroup decides upon a team name and a captain. The teacher or counselor then specifies the assignment, which is to use the materials to illustrate concepts that have been learned. For example, a group of ecology students might find a picture of recyclable goods. The activity should be conducted so as to stress small-group cooperation. The students may be timed or given a time-limit to complete the task; however, as with the educational-diagnostic meeting, the students should *not* be graded on their performances. Cooperative and qualitative aspects may be highlighted by having the students display their work, following the format of an art show. One of the subgroup members may be asked to describe to the entire class what the subgroup's posters illustrate, or each person may describe his own contribution. The students and teacher then identify which areas require further study and which students seem to need the help of others in the area of learning that was assessed. Needless to say, the active participation of the class members makes this particular type of meeting a welcome variation from the usual discussion. Usually, students and teachers develop further variations of how to use the materials and the game to meet other educational objectives.

To be effective, classroom meetings should become a part of the regular school program. Elementary school children could have them daily for fifteen to twenty minutes. High school students could have them at least two or three times per week for approximately thirty minutes. The classroom meeting is a major procedure for making school more relevant for students, building student involvement in learning, and helping students succeed rather than fail.

## FEELINGS CLASSES

Feelings classes are closely related to the concept of confluent education—the flowing together of the cognitive, the affective, and even the conative aspects of human learning and development. Feelings classes, as described by Faust (1968), should not be confused with sensitivity training. The main purpose of feelings classes is to give attention to the affective development of students and thereby to promote more involvement by students in their own intellectual and physical development. More specifically, feelings classes focus on the following main ideas: (1) many kinds of feelings exist; (2) nearly everybody experiences all the different feelings; (3) it is all right to have these feelings; (4) having a feeling is different from expressing a feeling; and (5) there are ways to express your feelings that are not harmful to yourself or others and, in many cases, these methods of expression are generally helpful. In an age characterized by national crime commissions studying the causes of violence, senseless wars, and the assassination of politicians, it might be wise to assist children in better accepting and expressing feelings.

Feelings buttons have been useful to help students realize that several types of feelings exist. These buttons have either facial expressions or words describing a particular feeling. The student wears the button that represents his feelings at the moment. Workbooks may also be centered around keeping a diary of the feelings the student had each day, why he had them, and what he did about them. Arithmetic lessons on fractions and percentages might include the feelings pie, which the student draws and divides into sections representing the way he feels. For example, he may choose to divide his pie into 50 percent happy, 15 percent sad, 15 percent joy, 10 percent angry, and 10 percent frustration. Students may draw or paint expressions of feelings. Magazine pictures, snapshots, and even baby pictures showing various expressions of feelings may be shared. Students can create additional materials for bulletin board displays.

Some classrooms maintain a feelings pillow or punching bag upon which children can vent some of their hostile feelings. One good way to create empathy for another person's situation is to role-play that person. Students may role-play people outside of class in much the same way they do creative drama.

The main point for the student to learn is that, although it is quite normal to experience a certain feeling, the manner in which the feeling is expressed is equally important. Although it is normal for one student to feel hate toward another student at times, hate is not best expressed by hitting the other person. The student may decide to release his energy through strenuous exercise and physical activity or to unload his anger by constructively confronting his tormentor.

Older students respond well to group discussions on how to change bad feelings. The school-counselor might ask students to describe what happens to them in connection with their feelings and behavior. Do feelings change without behavior change? Can a bad feeling be dispelled without changing behavior? If so, how? These questions facilitate group interaction about feelings. The group can share ideas on how feelings either block or facilitate personal development. Group feedback not only provides a standard of comparison for each member but also serves as a mirror of how one is affected by the expression of feelings.

An exciting unit for "slow learners" in tenth-grade English has been developed (Brown 1971). The unit includes a variety of activities which literally make the play, *Death of a Salesman*, come alive. The ten-minute touch conversation (p. 74) is an example of the verbal and nonverbal role-playing used in the lessons:

> *Procedure:* Form dyads; close eyes while standing. Using only your hands,
> 1. Carry on a conversation with the other person.
> 2. Slowly get acquainted.
> 3. One speaks, the other listens; then switch.
> 4. Do a dance together.
> 5. Have a fight.
> 6. Make up slowly. Don't hurry this.
> 7. Say good-bye.

Another communication exercise begins with partners talking face-to-face for three minutes, then standing back-to-back for three minutes while continuing to talk, and finally returning to eye-to-eye contact while continuing the communication *without words* for a final three-minute period. Another easy way to begin nonverbal communication skills is to have dyad partners tell each other a non-verbal story. Why is it important to focus on nonverbal communication? Some studies indicate that nonverbal communication makes up the greater part of messages, having much more impact than words alone (Mehrabian 1967). Frankly, words sometimes seem to provide impermeable blocks to expressions of true feeling. Nonverbal communication has a way of cutting through the verbal smog and smoke-screens used to cover real inner feelings. Sometimes it is helpful for a counselor to emulate the posture of a student he is counseling in order to have a more complete understanding of the student's feelings.

Before beginning feelings classes, teachers and counselors would do well to consider Greer and Rubenstein's idea (1972) of "warm-up" games for classroom activities. Warm-up helps students make the transition from their world to schooling by getting the students involved in a ritualistic activity.

So much has been written about feelings classes that games and techniques abound. Perhaps one of the best ways to personalize feelings discussions is to become involved in *measuring ourselves*. The best description of the techniques of *measuring ourselves* is presented by John Holt (1970). Students might measure their pulse while sleeping, walking, or exercising. The effects of anxiety and anger on pulse-rate might be determined. Likenesses and differences might be recorded and awards given for lowest and highest pulse-rates under various conditions.

Measuring ourselves need not stop there; respiration, blood pressure, and galvanic skin response are especially good indicators of emotional stress, anxiety, anger, and fear. Some of these indicators might be used to help students desensitize themselves to certain fears and situations.

Much criticism has been leveled at the various "affective" programs used in school settings by school-counselors or teachers. One reason may be that the whole area of affective learning has been unrelated to the study of the physical self. The more students understand about the interrelationships of body, feelings, and thoughts, the more relevant would the learning appear to be.

The counselor and teacher should plan activities that assist students in learning and understanding the feelings-class concept.

Brown (1971), Anandam, Davis, and Poppen (1971), and Weinstein and Fantini (1970) present several strategies designed for encouraging learning about feelings.

Not everyone agrees with the objectives for feelings classes. Those who oppose feelings classes say there is a danger in concentrating on the expression of hate and anger feelings. Support for this viewpoint comes from research findings showing that people who express feelings of anger are more likely to increase rather than decrease the frequency of such behavior. The argument is that if anger begets anger, an individual would do well to examine more closely the things he tells himself that make him so angry in the first place.

Two persons frequently react quite differently to what appears to be the same stimulus event because of what each tells himself about the event (Ellis 1969). For example, two students are standing in line. Harold arrives on the scene and pushes ahead of both of the students. One of the students tells himself: "I'm annoyed with Harold for pushing his way into the line. While this is bad, it's certainly not one of the worst things in the world, but I do want to talk to him about this." The other student might tell himself different things about the same incident: "That guy can't get away with crowding ahead of me in line. He's trying to make me look bad in front of my friends and that's *really* bad. Well, he's gone too far this time!" A fight breaks out and continues until broken up by a teacher or the principal.

Ellis recommends an approach to emotional education that forces attention on the differing reactions people have to the same or similar events. Each of the students above had the option of one of two thoughts: (1) "I don't like Harold's crowding in front of me. I *wish* he wouldn't." (2) "I can't *stand* Harold's crowding in. That's terrible!" Ellis's emotional-education program is directed toward having the counselor and students examine the relationship between emotion and thinking. The emphasis is upon action based upon rational thought rather than responding to illogical thinking such as: "I should be loved and admired by everyone I meet. If not, life is awful."

## GUIDELINES FOR GROUP LEADERS

Several types of counseling groups have been mentioned, all of which have value for the school-counselor. An effective group counselor should have knowledge of at least three areas: (1) group-counseling philosophy, (2) group-member behavior, and (3) group-leadership behavior.

## Group-Counseling Philosophy

*Self-Disclosure.* Developing closeness or cohesiveness among group members is more important than unmasking the group members to a point where they are overly vulnerable. The first purpose is to establish communication lines between group members. Self-disclosure should be developed to a point where the group is able to share present feelings and thoughts—particularly as these relate to other group members. Most of the focus is "here and now" and the past is related only when it connects to present behavior, feelings, and thoughts.

*Honesty.* For each group member, honesty is the value he places on his own actions. Valuing his behavior involves what he feels and thinks about what he does. Valuing involves examining what seems to make sense in his life and what style of life he pursues. The group offers each member the opportunity to share his internal view of life as well as his more obvious external expressions of self.

*Responsibility.* Each group member is assumed to be responsible for himself and his behavior in the group.

*Choices.* Generally, the choices are either an extension or a regression of personal growth and development. The group members may advance or retreat when making personal choices.

*Feedback.* Learning in groups is directly related to the amount of feedback accepted by group members. Through feedback from fellow group members and by personal evaluation of his own behavior, each group member increases his understanding of himself and his behavior.

*Decisions.* Decisions are of two types: personal and group. Personal decision-making can utilize the resources of other group members. Decisions made by the group require everyone's participation.

## Group-Member Behavior

*Gossiping.* Gossiping outside the group is not helpful and whatever is said within the group should be confidential. No one should repeat what is said *in* the group *outside* of the group unless it concerns himself only. Within the group, members may talk only about those persons who are present and should communicate directly with group members. In other words, no gossip is allowed within the group either. When a member does not direct his talk to a particular person, the group leader should ask, "To whom are you saying this?" The group members are encouraged to make a distinction between *talking to* and *talking at* other group members.

*Listening.* Everyone in the group is encouraged to listen to both the content and the feeling being expressed by other group members. When listening becomes difficult, the listener has a responsibility to inform the speaker of this fact in order to relieve his own boredom.

*Criticizing.* Criticism of a group member should be directed only to those things the group member can change—the *here, now, what,* and *how.*

Moving from the *why* toward the *what* and *how* of a member's behavior keeps the attention away from endless rationalization of ineffective past behavior.

*Intellectualizing.* Group members are encouraged to disclose "shareable" thoughts and feelings that are personal. Discussions revolving around social issues and politics remove attention from the individuals within the group and are more appropriate for classes and general discussion groups. Talking about something one of the group members likes becomes more meaningful when he describes his complete feelings about it, indicates how important its value is to him, and states how he acts in accordance with this value.

*Questioning.* Questions are generally discouraged because many questions are actually statements. When a member attempts to ask a question, he should be encouraged to rephrase it as a statement. For example, questions such as, "Don't you think we should... ?" are usually statements "I think we should . . . !"

*Leveling.* Especially helpful in groups are those members who express themselves (as much as possible) as they really are and really feel. Each member should become aware of his bodily reactions and use these as clues to determine his honest reactions to people and their behavior.

*I Language.* Group members are reminded to use *I* language. "I really felt silly when . . ." "I never do that sort of . . ." *instead of* "One just doesn't do that sort of . . ." Each member is encouraged to own his thoughts, feelings, and behaviors. Using the third-person *it* is another way a member may attempt to disassociate himself from his behavior. And it may be more honest to replace phrases such as "I can't" with "I won't."

*Make a Guess.* "I don't know" may be an avoidance behavior. Any member saying "I don't know" should make a guess or state how things would be changed if he knew. A group member may find it helpful to identify what he *avoids* in the group and to guess how his avoidance behavior rewards him.

*Shouldisms.* "Shouldisms" impede a group member's progress. Thinking "It is this way," *rather than* "It should be this way," is encouraged.

*Thinking and Feeling.* Group members are encouraged to separate what they *think* from what they *feel:* "I think we are . . ." *instead of* "I feel we need to . . ." By putting the two together, the member says, "I *think* the group is blocked and this makes me *feel* frustrated."

### Group-Leadership Behavior

*Facilitating.* All group leaders attempt to utilize to a greater or lesser extent the resources in the group. Facilitating requires the leader to assess the existing abilities within the group and to function in such a way as to let things develop from the group. Sharing, supporting, deciding, and learning are all group activities that will occur naturally if the leader allows the members to take the lead.

*Initiating.* Every group leader is somewhat active and initiates group activity. Some leaders plan a considerable amount of activity, and function much like an orchestra leader by telling members what to do next. The extent to which the group leader attempts to "make things happen" varies and is dependent upon many factors, such as the type of group, the size of the group, and the "style" of the leader.

*Intervening.* At times the leader must decide whether to intervene in group interaction and in what way to intervene. A group leader might intervene to protect the right of a group member to be heard or to block what he considers to be destructive feedback. The leader also intervenes in such simple ways as keeping time and closing the meetings, although some group leaders utilize alarm clocks for this purpose.

*Rule-keeping.* The group leader usually states various rules, which he intends for the group to follow. The leader may actively enforce the rules or encourage group members to check up on each other. Rule-keeping may be viewed as a special type of intervention in group interaction.

*Modeling.* The group leader demonstrates the kind of behavior appropriate in the group setting. For example, the group leader might make a personal self-disclosure as a way to show group members the type of sharing and expression possible in the group.

*Counseling.* The group leader may function as a counselor to individuals both inside and outside the group. Rules about counseling individuals outside the group are usually stated at the beginning of the group. The content of individual counseling is usually considered appropriate for discussion within the entire group and the rules of "gossip" also apply to individual counseling.

For a number of reasons, school-counselors are becoming more familiar with group approaches and more skilled in group leadership. Groups are proving to be an economical means of providing counseling to more students; moreover, group counseling is deemed superior to individual counseling in helping students resolve problems relating to peer relationships and social behavior.

## REFERENCES

Anandam, K.; Davis, M.; and Poppen, W. 1971. "Feelings . . . to Fear or to Free?" *Elementary School Guidance and Counseling* 5:181-89.

Blocher, D. 1966. *Developmental Counseling.* New York: Ronald Press.

Brown, G. 1971. *Human Teaching for Human Learning: An Introduction to Confluent Education.* New York: Viking Press.

Ellis, A. 1969. "Teaching Emotional Education in the Classroom." *School Health Review* 1:10-13.

Faust, V. 1968. *The Counselor-Consultant in the Elementary School.* Boston: Houghton-Mifflin.

Foreman, M.; Poppen, W.; and Frost, J. 1967. "Case Groups: An Inservice Education Technique." *Personnel and Guidance Journal* 46:388-92.

Glasser, W. 1969. *Schools Without Failure.* New York: Harper & Row.

Greer, M., and Rubinstein, B. 1972. *Will the Real Teacher Please Stand Up?* Pacific Palisades, Calif.: Goodyear Publishing.

Holt, J. 1970. *What Do I Do Monday?* New York: Dutton.

Hunter, E. 1972. *Encounter in the Classroom.* New York: Holt, Rinehart & Winston.

Mehrabian, A. 1967. "Orientation Behaviors and Nonverbal Attitude Communication." *Journal of Communication* 17:324-32.

Missildine, W. 1963. *Your Inner Child of the Past.* New York: Simon & Schuster.

Otto, H. 1967. *Guide to Developing Your Potential.* New York: Charles Scribner's Sons.

Raths, L.; Harmin, M.; and Simon, S. 1966. *Values and Teaching.* Columbus: Charles E. Merrill.

Sax, S., and Hollander, S. 1972. *Reality Games.* New York: Macmillan.

Simon, S. 1972. "The Teacher Education and Value Development." *Phi Delta Kappan* 53:649-51.

Thompson, C., and Poppen, W. 1972. *For Those Who Care: Ways of Relating to Youth*. Columbus: Charles E. Merrill.

Toffler, A. 1970. *Future Shock*. New York: Random House.

Von Hilsheimer, G. 1970. *How to Live with Your Special Child*. Washington: Acropolis.

Weinberg, G. 1969. *The Action Approach*. Cleveland: World.

Weinstein, G. and Fantini, M. 1970. *Toward Humanistic Education: A Curriculum of Affect*. New York: Praeger.

Welch, R. 1971. "A Weight Loss Program for Overweight Adolescent Girls and Its Effects on Self-Concepts." Unpublished dissertation, University of Tennessee, Knoxville.

Yalom, I. 1970. *The Theory and Practice of Group Psychotherapy*. New York: Basic Books.

# CHAPTER 5

# Noncounseling Functions of the School-Counselor

School-counselors do not counsel students all day. Counseling is hard work, and to counsel continuously, even for a short period of time, would be extremely difficult. Thus, while counseling is the school-counselor's primary function, he is also assigned other duties. These noncounseling activities, meaningful and important in themselves, serve to support and complement both the counseling function and the learning environment provided in the school.

Perhaps counselors have for too long devoted themselves to counseling students with problems, attempting to help them survive or succeed in a faulty school system, instead of performing various noncounseling functions that would improve the educational experience.

Much has been said about the school-counselor's role as it relates to teachers, parents, and administrators. Discussion of the counselor's role has resulted in a debate about whether the school-counselor is primarily a counselor of students or a consultant for teachers and other adults of significance to students. As the authorities choose up sides on this issue, it becomes clear that the debate cannot be resolved by an "either-or" solution. It is fruitless to argue whether the counselor should function only as a counselor or only as a consultant. School-counselors have a number of noncounseling functions that are necessary to support the counseling services provided to students.

Students need information about careers and colleges if they are to make decisions about their future vocations. Students benefit by understanding how people grow and develop psychologically as well as physically. Students benefit if their teachers and parents receive effective consultation from counselors about relating to youth. The counselor can influence the environment of youth as well as help individual young persons to resolve their inner conflicts. Techniques

100

of conflict-resolution and improving human relationships can be taught to both youth and the adults who work with youth. These are some of the noncounseling functions that might be performed by the school-counselor.

The noncounseling functions can easily be understood by determining what teachers and other adults need and want from a school-counselor. For example, teachers want someone who can help them *clarify* their concerns and develop new *behaviors*. Counselors are well aware that the initial problem statements of counselees are frequently not the real concerns. Similarly, teachers, parents, and administrators will present many pseudorequests to the counselor. The counselor, then, does not respond to every problem predetermined by the teacher. Rather, the counselor's task is to help teachers determine concerns and establish priorities. Such a task requires of the counselor both counseling skills and consultative expertise. In other words, while the school-counselor is consulting with the significant adults in a student's life, he continues to incorporate a counseling posture—he should not adopt the all too prevalent consultative stance of aloofness, remoteness, or assumed superiority.

What are some of the major noncounseling functions? Several are listed below. They are not presented in any order of priority. Rather it is assumed that each school-counselor or group of school-counselors will determine which of these functions have priority in their particular school setting. It is further assumed that counselors will not make this decision alone but will be responsive to the demands of students, parents, teachers, and administrators. All together will determine the priorities among the noncounseling roles of the school-counselor.

## THE COUNSELOR AS PSYCHOLOGICAL EDUCATOR

Psychological education is one noncounseling role that cannot be ignored. Psychological education has come to be called by many names, such as deliberate psychological education, affective learning, and mental health programs. Nearly all approaches stress classroom learning activities that help students more effectively to utilize their abilities in day-to-day living. Some label psychological education as a relatively new discipline (Ivey and Alschuler 1973), while others view it as a revival of a much older movement for classroom guidance in the curriculum of the school. Regardless of whether it is new or old, psychological education is intended to prevent problems rather than provide therapy for those who develop problems.

It is a major assumption of psychological education that love, hate, fear, anger, and joy, as very human emotions, affect the way learning and development occur. Children and youth must learn to accept these emotions and feelings in themselves and others and to be aware that it is normal to feel such emotions as hate and anger. Furthermore, children and youth need to learn "appropriate" ways for expressing these feelings—ways that do not infringe upon the rights of others, or inhibit their own growth and development.

What are the approaches to psychological education? As is usually the case with new movements, psychological education has brought with it a proliferation of terms, materials, and practices. Feelings classes, *T*-groups, encounter groups, growth groups, sensitivity training, and human development programs are some of the labels used for classroom activities dealing with affective learning. These are the *direct* approaches for promoting emotional growth. Many indirect approaches occur as a part of race relations projects, intergroup relations programs, group guidance, and mental health practices. Role-playing, feelings buttons, hostile pillows, magic carpets, and quiet corners are some of the tools and techniques of psychological education.

Complete programs of psychological education are based upon the developmental needs of youth and are designed to increase students' ability to foresee problems, determine alternatives, and effect decisions. Numerous programs have been developed, which systematically teach students a variety of interpersonal and personal skills. Psychological education is conducted in one of two ways: either the counselor personally teaches a course to groups of students, or he consults with teachers in order to get them to incorporate psychological education in the regular curriculum.

The impetus for the recent upsurge of psychological-education programs derived from a federally funded research project conducted at Harvard University. The project at Harvard was based upon "learning psychology by doing psychology," and had three components. One component, the counseling-psychology class, taught high school students the skills of peer counseling and actually had the students counsel some of their classmates. The second component was a class in educational psychology, which included practical experience in teaching younger children through an approach called cross-age tutoring. The third component was a study of early childhood psychology, in which high school students functioned as teacher-aides in a nursery school. These three classes are examples of what is done in psychological education. Other classroom applications utilize group-dynamics techniques, self-study, behavior modification, study of morals and values, programs in creativity, sensory awareness, decision-making, self-assessment, meditation, and biofeedback. There is considerable competition among the variations of psychological education because more and more psychological and counseling theories are being translated into layman's terms. In effect, a good psychological-education program attempts to train students in counseling skills so that the students can use these skills for their own personal development and interpersonal relations.

The counselor is in a unique position in the school because he has more background and training in psychology and counseling than the other members of the faculty usually possess. Consequently, if psychological education is provided to the students, it is often because the school-counselor functions in the noncounseling role of psychological educator.

## THE COUNSELOR AS CAREER EDUCATOR

Nearly all historians of the guidance and counseling movement include the vocational-guidance activities of Frank Parsons in Boston during the early 1900s as the origin of much of what is now school guidance and counseling. The National Vocational Guidance Association was formed in 1913 and has since become a part of the larger American Personnel and Guidance Association. Career or vocational guidance has existed through periods of high regard and periods of disrepute, and presently seems to be riding a high crest of popularity.

Since school-counselors, in at least one sense, have their origins in vocational guidance, and because a consistent high priority is assigned to career guidance by members of business and government, the school-counselor frequently acts as career educator. Career education does more than provide vocational counseling to students. Rather, it implies a systematic and sequential program of educational experiences for all students in grades K-12 or 14. Career education is designed to assist all students, whether they intend to enter college, post-high school vocational programs, high school vocational programs, or general education programs. Modern career education programs are designed to provide for career development, which is defined more completely as "life planning" or planning for a "style of life" (Wrenn 1973). With such a definition in mind, career education becomes a task much too large for counselors alone. Teachers, students, community resources, and counselors all have vital roles to play in offering a sequential "life-planning" program to all students.

As a career educator the counselor may teach some students directly, but the usual procedure is for the counselor to function as a coordinator of career-guidance activities conducted by teachers or other persons as a part of the regular school curriculum. In some cases the school-counselor does not coordinate the program but functions as a resource to the career-guidance activities. In other words, the counselor assists those working in career guidance to identify school and community resources available to assist children and youth in learning about the world of work and their own personal values, aspirations, and abilities.

In many instances, school systems employ counselors called career-counselors who are primarily responsible for career and vocational guidance. A career-counselor, as opposed to a school-counselor, may spend nearly all of his time performing the noncounseling function of career guidance. The reason for the specialized career-counselor is that a more generalized school-counselor frequently has little time available for career-guidance activities. School-counselors have also been criticized for not placing enough emphasis upon the developmental and motivational aspects of career planning and consequently placing too much emphasis on specific job choice, short-term counseling, and aptitude testing.

| CAREER-GUIDANCE PROGRAM OBJECTIVES | ACTIVITIES |
| --- | --- |
| Develop positive self-concepts | Self-study units in curriculum |
| Positive attitude toward work | "Hands-on" experience with workers, tools, and equipment |
| Increase knowledge of work-world | Direct-observation field trips |
| Decrease dropouts and occupational stereotypes | Special speakers and programs relating to minorities and women in work-world |
| Increase job-application skills | Simulated experiences in job application |
| Better job-placement and satisfaction | Summer counselor workshop with industry and employment agencies; follow-up counseling for graduates |

Listed in the left-hand column of the accompanying table are some of the objectives common to a complete program of career or vocational guidance. In the right-hand column are listed some of the activities used to achieve these objectives.

The table illustrates that the modern concept of career guidance is a program too broad to be accomplished by either elementary-school or secondary-school counselors alone. The school-counselor who perceives the developmental tasks of youth and realizes the significance of "career choice" in contemporary society, will work actively to promote a sequential program of career-guidance activities at all levels of schooling.

## THE COUNSELOR AND TESTING

Lyman (1968) has reported that more than one million standardized tests are given each day to children in American schools. Such tests are generally used even if the school does not employ a counselor. Yet in schools that do employ counselors, the counselor is usually involved with either the administration of the tests or the interpretation of the test results. School-counselors are trained to utilize standardized test results appropriately for the benefit of the students. Even when the counselor is not assigned some responsibility for the standardized testing program, some involvement will develop because the counselor may want to decrease misuse and abuse of standardized test results. No less an authority than Henry S. Dyer, Vice-President of Educational Testing Service, noted, in a speech in 1971, that few educators seem aware of the limitations of the results of testing. Dyer went on to detail how I.Q.'s and grade-equivalency scores are among the devices that cause many teachers and perhaps some administrators to completely misconstrue the meaning of a student's test performance.

Why are tests given? Tests are administered, scored, and interpreted for a number of reasons. One purpose is to enable school administrators to have information about the students they are responsible for educating. Knowledge of the average intelligence and the range of intelligence among the students should give the school administration some idea of how to modify educational offerings. Achievement tests can also serve teachers and administrators in evaluating the school curriculum. For example, if classes in the school consistently score low in reading achievement, increased resources and effort might be put into reading instruction. In other words, tests should help to determine whether certain subject areas are assigned too low an instructional priority and whether enrichment of some kind may be required.

Test results can also be used to evaluate new instructional methods to determine whether they are as effective or more effective than the previous curriculum. Some schools have found, for example, that scores in mathematical computation decreased as a result of introducing modern mathematics (the "new math"). Some of the teachers thought that the lower scores were only a temporary depression resulting from adopting a new program. Later testing showed, though, that the scores remained low even after the teachers were very familiar with the modern mathematics. Consequently, the mathematics program was enriched with additional computational exercises and the scores returned to the previous level, which was approximately average for the age and grade.

Achievement test scores can also be utilized to help teachers plan instructional programs for individual students. In order to do so, it is necessary that the teacher be informed of the students' right and wrong responses by item. An analysis of each student's individual-item responses is quite expensive and time-consuming; however, it is necessary if the teacher is to determine exactly what a particular student needs to study in order to improve his achievement.

Other tests are used to screen and place students in classes for exceptional children, such as the mentally retarded, the emotionally disturbed, and those who have learning disabilities or other handicaps. Testing for special-program placement or selection usually is reserved for the school psychologist or psychological examiner.

Another purpose of testing is to benefit the student and increase his self-understanding. In some cases students may want test information to help them make a decision about which college to enter, what high school courses to take, or which general vocational area to pursue. Test results are, of course, only one of many considerations when making a decision of such magnitude. In most cases, school testing programs are designed to help administrators and teachers more than students. Students would be better served, too, if the tests used for decision-making were taken recently, and if the counselor who interpreted the test was also aware of the procedures of test administration.

Standardized testing programs do not provide individualized and recent test data. They are multipurpose, intended to meet the diverse needs of administrators, teachers, and students. Multipurpose tests frequently serve none of these purposes well. It would behoove the school-counselor to involve himself with school testing pro-grams at least to the extent of assuring their appropriate use. In order to do so, the school-counselor must understand the basic principles of testing and measurement. Barry and Wolf (1962), present the fol-lowing generalizations, which might guide not only school-counselors but other consumers of test data—administrators, teachers, and students:

1. Individual tests are usually better indicators of student intelligence and achievement than group tests. Individualized testing is much more time-consuming and not without error; however, it is generally more comprehensive and accurate than standardized tests given to large groups of students.

2. Even the best test is never more than a sample of how a stu-dent performs; therefore, the test score is subject to sampling error. Test scores are best considered as an estimate rather than an absolute score. Because of sampling error, it is im-possible to predict, for example, whether a student who scored as much as ten or even fifteen points higher than another student on a test will outscore the other student again. If the same two students are retested, the student with the lower score on the first test may well obtain the higher score on the second testing.

3. Predictions about individual behavior are especially risky. Predictions are somewhat accurate for groups of students but little better than guesswork for individuals. Consider, for example, how often the favorite horse in a race is upset and how often a "long shot" wins. Predicting that persons with low test scores will not succeed is much like predicting that "long shots" will not win sporting events. The fact is that long shots do win, and people with low test scores do succeed at least frequently enough to make prediction of success or failure a risky business.

4. Test scores become less accurate with age. The score a stu-dent received in the tenth grade is less likely to indicate how he is functioning in the twelfth grade than a test taken when he is in the twelfth grade. Moreover, older tests reflect the culture of the time during which they were written and there-fore may incorporate testing concepts no longer relevant to a child's experience. Tests with recent publication dates are more likely to contain items related to the experiences of today's youth than tests with a publication date of eight to ten years ago.

There are other factors to consider about standardized testing in the schools: for example, no test is culture free, and most tests measure whether a child has learned the vocabulary, beliefs, and rules of middle-class American society.

Other issues confront the consumer of standardized tests. Are test results misused by the release of scores to parents and the public? Can teachers and teacher-aides be expected to keep test scores confidential? Are test results properly interpreted or is misinformation often presented to students by both counselors and teachers? Does the use of some types of test constitute a violation of privacy and personal rights? (What is more personal than one's I.Q. score?)

Testing is and has been subjected to considerable criticism; at times it has even been considered part of a Communist plot (Barclay 1968). Yet testing—in fact, considerable testing—is conducted in the schools, and the school-counselor has little choice but to become as skilled and conversant as possible about tests so that he can see that they are given only for appropriate purposes and that the results are used responsibly.


## THE COUNSELOR AS PARENT EDUCATOR

Although the counselor's work is often thought to be only with students and teachers, there is a need for working with parents in a number of situations. Lipsman (1969) prophesies that now and in the future the counselor is going to be working more with community resources outside of the school setting. "If our goal is to release potential for learning and self-actualization, we must extend our field to where major obstructions reside . . . parental attitudes and expectations, family values . . ." (p. 100). The counselor must ask himself, "Where will my intervention be most effective?" Many school-counselors conclude that being a consultant to parents is an important noncounseling function.

McCowan (1968), in his study of under-achievers, found that working with parents was more effective in improving the achievement of students than counseling the students themselves. Although it is possible to make only limited generalizations from these findings, they do illustrate the important role parents can play in affecting student behavior. Most counselors choose to work with groups of parents, pointing out the economy of working with groups. The same thirty minutes needed to consult privately with only one parent may be more wisely used by working with a group of parents.

In addition to the economy argument, it is believed that things can be accomplished in groups that are impossible in a one-to-one counselor-parent relationship. Parents meeting in groups find support in the fact that they share common problems and concerns. The group setting also has a facilitating effect on the development of communication skills. Poor communication often causes imbalances in the parent-child relationship, and learning to express oneself clearly is seen as an important by-product of the group setting.

If the counselor does decide that working with parents might be profitable in a particular situation, what variables should be examined before undertaking the task? Shaw (1973, p. 105) explored the feasibility of working with parent groups in the elementary school setting. His study shows two variables to be of major importance in influencing the amount of parent participation. The first factor is the socioeconomic and ethnic composition of the school. As a rule, middle-class white schools have the highest amount of parent participation. The other factor is the principal's attitude toward consultation services and activities. If the principal advocates extensive use of the school-counselor's services, parent participation is greater.

## A PRACTICAL MODEL FOR PARENT CONSULTATION

If the counselor surveys his situation and decides that parent groups could be effective, how does he begin? Poppen (1968) developed a group process for working with teachers concerned about children who displayed oppositional behaviors in the classroom. The process has been adapted for working with parent groups. It consists of three phases:

1. A presentation concerning the systematic observation of children's behavior. A brief lecture illustrates to parents what has proved helpful to other parents who had concerns about one or more of their children. A plan is presented by which group members can observe their own behaviors and the behaviors of their children.
2. Voluntary presentation of problem situations by parents. The most helpful method seems to be the presentation of one or two situations per session. Two important guidelines are followed during the case presentation: (1) little talk about past history is accepted—what is important is what is happening now; (2) there are no experts in the group to give

advice, only people who develop "action plans" that seem feasible to the parent. This process helps the parent view more objectively and realistically exactly what his child is doing and what he (the parent) is doing about it.

3. Concentration on discussion of the underlying needs that may be prompting the child to behave in a particular way. In effect, the parents attempt to identify the "payoff" the child receives for behaving in a certain way.

Critical elements in assuring that learning and behavior change occur in the group are feedback and recycling. Each group member should review his plan and its enactment before the group at each meeting. Plans are occasionally inappropriate and frequently are incorrectly implemented. Sometimes the plans are not enacted, and provisions must be made to insure that first attempts are made by the parents.

Parents are also allowed to examine and better understand their own feelings about themselves as parents, especially the feelings they have in response to their child's behavior.

Gordon (1970) has developed a program of parent effectiveness training. It is a laboratory or workshop course intended to effect changes in parental attitudes and to develop skills and techniques for putting these changed attitudes into practice. The course consists of twenty-four hours of classroom instruction and a workbook designed to help in applying the newly learned skills in the home.

The major premise upon which the program is based is a theory of healthy relationships, which is formulated on a framework of experiential or client-centered counseling. The basic theoretical framework of the parent effectiveness program applies not only to parent-child relationships, but to all interpersonal relationships.

The school-counselor should become thoroughly familiar with the theory underlying whatever approach he uses in consulting with parents. In initiating a program for parents, it would also be advisable to enlist the services of interested professionals in the community. Once a group of parents becomes familiar with the program, they may serve as instructors for future groups.

Parents have long been one of the "excuses" the school has used to rationalize its ineffectiveness, and there probably are some parents who are a hindrance rather than a help to the child in his learning. The common practice of having parents help the pupil with homework is doomed to failure if the parent has a negative attitude toward homework and learning. In fact, such a practice may inadvertently be reinforcing the child's distaste for school work. Another common occurrence is that a report to parents that their son or daughter is "hard to handle" is interpreted as a command to "shape-up" your child. Consequently, they assure the teacher that they will go right home and give him a good spanking. In either case, *extensive* parent education is in order. One of the models presented in this chapter may be useful to the school-counselor who wishes to initiate a parent-education program.

## THE COUNSELOR AS HUMANIZING FORCE IN THE SCHOOL

School-counselors are becoming aware that resolutions to problems do not always reside within the students. Many students can be helped most by humanizing the environment wherein they live. When the counselor functions as a force for change in this area, the ecological system rather than the student receives the emphasis. The counselor attempts to manipulate the environment in order to make it a place where people would want to be. There are a number of ways that counselors can attempt to modify learning and living environments. Some school-counselors use a systems approach (Peters 1972), become change agents (Cook 1971), or function as psychoecologists (Kuriloff 1973). Another approach, which will be described here more fully, is for the counselor to attempt to modify the transactions between people and alleviate faulty transactions. This approach might also be referred to as role-shifting or experimenting. The most practical presentation of this approach is probably that of David Keirsey (1968). Briefly, the idea is that if a person begins playing a new role (behaving differently), those around him will react differently. For example, if a teacher plays the role of observing a child's behavior instead of nagging him, the child will stop his misbehavior because his misbehavior is no longer being reinforced. This approach is rather direct, with the counselor merely telling someone to try out a new role. What the role will be is not crucial. In fact, Keirsey says, "If I don't know what role to put somebody in, I pick one at random, on the premise that almost any role is better than the one that is now being played in certain situations" (p. 39). There are, however, some general ideas which can help the counselor determine a role to prescribe.

One idea is to identify the role presently being played and change to the opposite behavior. For example, an overdirective teacher may become a "helpless bystander" to an inactive or resistive pupil. At times it is helpful to play one's present role, but to gain intensity by exaggerating it. Those around the exaggerating role-player may become more aware of the problem in the relationship and consequently modify their behavior. For example, the "good teacher," who does too much caretaking of students, may find them becoming more self-reliant after repeated attempts to be overly help-ful and to do everything for them.

There are a number of ways to get people to enact a role-shift other than by simply suggesting a new role. Many times people will play a new role as a means of gathering data or assisting the coun-selor in "diagnostic activities." When people watch the behavior of those around them, they automatically adopt a new role for them-selves—scientific observer. Teachers are especially willing to try new roles for the sake of experimentation, so much so that one way to promote positive change is through action-research projects within the school. Kagan (1971) points out that enacting curriculum changes often has more beneficial effects upon the teacher than upon the students. What may, in fact, be happening is that the teacher adopts a new interest in the content of the curriculum and, at least for a while, adopts the role of a learner rather than a teacher. Perhaps another way of expressing this idea might be to "program" teachers for at least some "fun" each day. Having teachers play the role of "fun-maker" works to assure that the teachers will maintain at least some interest in teaching.

Another specific technique, which is quite consistent with the role-shifting approach, is the use of interaction analysis (Amidon and Flanders 1967) as a means of helping teachers improve com-munication in the classroom. Systems for analyzing both verbal and nonverbal interaction exist. Essentially what is indicated from the research of Amidon and others is that the "indirect" teacher is more effective than the teacher using direct influence as the basic mode of classroom communication. The interaction analysis is a feedback system, which should prove helpful to the counselor who hopes to be able to help teachers shift to more indirect teaching roles.

An elementary-school counselor, hoping to be a humanizing force in the school, might become quite involved in the placement of pupils in the primary grades. The counselor would assess the child behaviorally and thereby determine the type of teacher most suited for the child. The behavioral assessment might occur during the kindergarten program or during small-group play settings at the beginning of the school year. Most frequently, pupils would be placed with teachers who have a personality style opposite that of the child's most significant adults—that is, mother, father, or next-older sibling. In implementing this placement program the counselor is, in effect, applying the research of Yondo and Kagan (1968), which indicates that the most effective technique for making an impulsive child more reflective or a reflective child more impulsive is to place the pupil with a teacher with the opposite "tempo." According to their research, the greatest changes among pupils occurred in impulsive boys who had reflective teachers with considerable experience. Any counselor interested in promoting this idea might also study the work of Thelen (1967).

The preceding was intended to present only a few methods of environmental manipulation. It is beyond the scope of this section to present all the ways the counselor might work as a force to improve the educational system. Finally, it is not suggested that school-counselors are alone responsible for promoting positive changes in schools. There are many other persons within the school and the community, including administrators, teachers, students, and parents, who are equally responsible.

## THE COUNSELOR AS IN-SERVICE EDUCATOR

Shaw (1973) has stated that many traditional counselors would be surprised to learn that in-service training is included as a function of the school-counselor. Presenting programs to assist teachers with their learning has become a frequent noncounseling role for the contemporary school-counselor.

If the premise that teachers teach as they are taught is accepted, sloppy in-service education cannot be afforded. If education is to change and be revitalized, in-service education is the logical place to begin. Learning situations for teachers must exemplify what is expected to happen in school classrooms. Those responsible for in-service education, especially the school-counselor, cannot preach one type of education for children and have another type for teachers. The old adage, "What you do speaks so loudly that I cannot hear what you say," is an appropriate motto for the school-counselor to remember when he functions as an in-service educator.

In-service education has a number of general objectives. Among these, the following are especially pertinent to the school-counselor:

1. To increase teacher understanding of the conditions that promote learning and the factors that influence the student in the

    learning process.

2. To develop teacher understanding of the dynamics of teacher-student relationships and to improve skills in communicating with youth.

3. To increase teacher skill in communicating with parents.

Theodore Sizer, Dean of Harvard's Graduate School of Education, has said, "There is nothing grimmer than the itinerant education professor lecturing late in the afternoon to exhausted teachers." Although such instruction happens with in-service education offerings and graduate classes, it certainly is not an ideal means of developing the teacher as a person—unless, of course, one finds suffering a growth experience. One extremely potent subject for in-service education is a study of what teachers do and how they can improve. Sizer says that "in-service education is probably best performed as internal reform and reshaping." He adds that "there is nothing more highly charged than a school system involved in continual self-evaluation and reform." A good in-service program can provide such reform, and the school-counselor can be a vital part of effective in-service education.

There are a number of activities the school-counselor can use to help teachers learn. Workshops can be organized to give teachers "hands-on" experience in learning about new materials, such as career-education materials, to be used in classrooms. Seminars might be planned to help teachers learn how to use grade- or behavior-contracting. Brainstorming meetings or "think shops" might be utilized to help teachers resolve a particular problem in dealing with a group of students or parents. Small-group meetings might be held in which teachers could discuss their relationships with students and how to improve them. Procedures may be used whereby teachers share ideas or learn from one another, perhaps by visiting another class or role-playing teaching situations.

Although some objectives and activities for in-service programs are suggested, it is not intended that a program of in-service activities should be forced upon teachers. Teachers must be involved in deciding on the objectives of their own in-service education. The purposes of the in-service activities must be directly related to the needs of the teachers and their school situation. A successful program seems assured if teachers understand their own problems, care about solving these problems, and become involved in planning their own learning experiences.

## OTHER NONCOUNSELING FUNCTIONS

There are other noncounseling roles that school-counselors might assume. The specific roles any counselor fills are determined by conditions and needs within his school and community. Some counselors become involved in drug-abuse and prevention programs, either by providing direct counseling to students with such problems, or by assisting teachers or parents in planning prevention programs. Similarly, some counselors work to initiate or support sex-education programs for students. Serving as directors or consultants to tutorial programs for students is another noncounseling function that became very popular during the late 1960s and early 1970s. Each of these functions is responsive to one of the many fads or temporary needs that develop from time to time in education. One strength of an effective school-counselor is that he is flexible enough to modify his role and function to satisfy existing conditions and needs.

There are other ways of viewing the activities of school-counselors, but they are beyond the scope of this book. For example, every counselor makes referrals to other sources. Every counselor performs some kind of public-relations activity, as do most other educational specialists. Karl Menninger, in *The Vital Balance*, pointed out that man has an "urge to classify things around him" and later to reclassify the same things in quite a different way. No doubt school-counselors and counselor-educators will treat noncounseling functions similarly for as long as counselors continue to have a place in the schools.

## REFERENCES

Amidon, E., and Flanders, N. 1967. *The Role of the Teacher in the Classroom: A Manual for Understanding and Improving Teachers' Classroom Behavior.* Minneapolis: P. S. Amidon and Associates.

Barclay, J. 1968. *Controversial Issues in Testing.* Boston: Houghton-Mifflin.

Barry, R., and Wolf, B. 1962. *Epitaph for Vocational Guidance.* New York: Teacher's College Press.

Cook, D. 1971. *Guidance for Education in Revolution.* Boston: Allyn & Bacon.

Gordon, T. 1970. *Parent Effectiveness Training.* New York: Peter H. Wyden.

Ivey, A., and Alschuler, A. 1973. "An Introduction to the Field." *Personnel and Guidance Journal* 51:591-97.

Kagan, G. 1971. *Understanding Children: Behavior, Motives and Thought.* New York: Harcourt Brace Jovanovich.

Keirsey, D. 1968. "Transactional Casework: Creative Counseling Techniques." In *Counseling: A Venture in Human Freedom,* ed. W. Maes, Temple, Ariz.: Bureau of Educational Research and Services, Arizona State University.

Kuriloff, P. 1973. "The Counselor as Psychoecologist." *Personnel and Guidance Journal* 51:321-27.

Lipsman, C. 1969. "Revolution and Prophecy: Community Involvement for Counselors." *Personnel and Guidance Journal* 48:97-100.

Lyman, H. 1968. *Intelligence, Aptitude and Achievement Testing.* Boston: Houghton-Mifflin.

McCowan, R. 1968. "Group Counseling with Underachievers and Their Parents." *School Counselor* 16:30-35.

Menninger, K. 1963. *The Vital Balance.* New York: Viking Press.

Peters, H. 1972. "Systems Approaches: Educational-Vocational Counseling." In *The Practice of Guidance,* ed. H. Peters, R. Dunlap, and R. Aubrey. Denver: Love Publishing Co.

Poppen, W. 1968. "Case Conference Groups as In-service Education Technique." Unpublished dissertation, Ohio State University.

Shaw, M. 1973. *School Guidance Systems.* Boston: Houghton-Mifflin.

Thelen, H. A. 1967. *Classroom Grouping for Teachability.* New York: John Wiley.

Wrenn, C. 1973. *The World of the Contemporary Counselor.* Boston: Houghton-Mifflin.

Yondo, R., and Kagan, J. 1968. "The Effect of Teacher Tempo on the Child." *Child Development* 39:27-34.

CHAPTER 6

# Issues, Trends, and Research
# in School Counseling

## MAJOR ISSUES AND TRENDS IN SCHOOL COUNSELING

This section presents some of the major issues commonly debated among professional school-counselors and counselor-educators. It should be noted that the basic issues do not seem to change considerably with time—rather, the changes occur in the positions taken on the issues. These positions, of course, are influenced by a number of factors—for example, the supply of counselors, the demand for counselors, the amount of federal support for counseling services, and current fads in education. Concerning the latter, some fads, such as career education, result in increased employment of counselors. Other fads, such as individualization of instruction, may reduce the need for counselors. Regardless of the changing influences upon education and school counseling, however, what appear to be the common issues and future trends in school counseling?

One issue is whether counseling should be provided for *all* students or only for students who have problems and request help? Those who advocate counseling for *all* students propose a developmental guidance program, which would reach out of the counselor's office into the classrooms and the curriculum. The counselor who proposes to serve all students must utilize the assistance of teachers, parents, and students. Group approaches are also used extensively. The group approach is advocated because it is economical and because in some ways it is more effective than individual counseling. Human relations training is offered both to prevent the development of problems and as a form of therapy for those with problems.

Few members of the counseling profession oppose the idea of counseling all students, except on the ground that it would be too expensive to implement. Those who advocate concentrating coun-

117

seling services among students with problems argue that it is better
to do counseling thoroughly for a few than superficially for all. The
debate really contrasts counseling as a therapeutic process with
counseling as an educational process. It is also argued against the
counseling-for-all-students idea that no real results can be demonstrated, whereas counselors who help a few students with problems
can demonstrate their effectiveness by keeping records of the problems they have helped eradicate.

Some counselor-educators, most notably Peters (1970), advance
the idea that intensive counseling should be provided for all students. In such programs there would be one counselor for every one
hundred students. Such counselor-student ratios rarely exist and will
not until counseling is supported at a very high level.

It appears that the trend is toward counseling for all students
because more systematic and programmatic counseling approaches
are being utilized. Peer counseling, which has considerable research
support, is one example of a recent innovation that is providing counseling for more students without extensive budget increases. Counseling skills are being "demystified"; more people are being trained.
Consequently, paraprofessionals, teachers, and parents are performing counseling functions for youth (Cowen 1971). While it is extremely
difficult to predict trends (forecasters are more frequently wrong
than right), it does appear, barring unforeseen circumstances, that
more counseling will be provided to more students. If, for some
reason, the peer, parent, and paraprofessional counseling programs
are mismanaged and breaches of confidentiality or ethics occur frequently, the paraprofessional counseling movement may do a quick
about-face, and the backlash will result in only a few counselors
working with a few students.

A second issue is whether school-counselors should be selected
primarily from the teaching profession or from among persons who
have all types of academic backgrounds. A common debate among
counselor-educators and school-counselors centers around the need
for teaching experience as a prerequisite to entrance into the school-
counseling profession. Nearly all state certification standards include
teaching experience as one of the requirements for becoming a school-
counselor. Consequently the debate is more academic than practical. The facts indicate that few school-counselors enter the profession without preparation in teaching and some teaching experience.

Those who argue against the teaching-experience requirement
say that there is little or no evidence to support the theory that teaching makes a person a better counselor. In fact, many counselor-

educators contend that because counseling and teaching are different activities, the experience of teaching impedes the development of a counselor. More simply stated, the language of teaching is viewed as the opposite of the language of counseling; therefore, prospective counselors who have been teachers need to undergo considerable "unlearning" of established language patterns. Persons without teaching experience are reportedly more open to the language of counseling; consequently, they can be more efficiently trained.

Additional discussion on the teaching-experience issue advances the idea that there is more to school counseling than conducting counseling interviews with students. In fact, as counselors begin to work more directly with teachers as consultants, the counselors' acceptance by teachers becomes more important. Teachers tend to view counselors with teaching experience as more credible than those who have not successfully managed a classroom of students on a day-to-day basis. School administrators also tend to view counselors with teaching experience as more trustworthy and more committed to the educational profession. Related arguments focus upon whether the counselor is basically a psychologist or an educator, and whether he primarily serves the institution or the students.

At the present time, certification standards require counselors to be quite committed to the educational profession and to the school as an institution. Until some other procedure is developed for selecting the best people for counseling, teaching experience will continue to be a part of school-counselor certification.

Those who argue against the teaching-experience requirement point out that many of the present counselors (who were recruited from teaching) are not effective and that personnel from other backgrounds might have been better counseling students and therefore better counselors. No doubt, talented, intelligent persons could function as effective counselors without teaching experience, and mere possession of teaching experience does not guarantee adequate counselor functioning.

A third major issue relates to the preparation of counselors for their profession. Should the stress be placed upon developing the counselor as a person or should emphasis be given to counselor's learning techniques and acquiring knowledge? Those who place greater priority on developing the counselor as a person argue that the counselor should experience considerable individual and group counseling as a client. Self-awareness and personal adjustment are deemed to be prerequisites for the acquisition of counseling knowledge and techniques. Extended to its logical conclusion, the argument for an experiential training program says in effect that what the counselor is, is more important than what he knows.

Hand in hand with this debate over type of preparation is the related concern about the degree to which personality or intellectual factors should be considered in selecting prospective students for schooling in counseling. Some counselor-educators place heavy emphasis upon the intellectual development of the school-counselor and favor students with a high academic performance or high academic aptitude. It is argued that what the school-counselor is as a person is inconsequential unless he has special knowledge and skills that can be used to assist students and teachers.

At times the debate over personal qualities and cognitive understanding seems meaningless! The school-counselor needs both to be effective. The issue can be compromised, but at the expense of extending the duration of the training program. While extended programs (a minimum of two years) are often proposed, few actually exist, and many practicing school-counselors oppose the idea. The dilemma appears practically insoluble. Programs to develop "ideal" counselors look good on the drawing-board, but people differ about what is "ideal" and products of "ideal" programs are still human and frequently err. No doubt the school-counseling profession will continue to employ a wide and diverse range of types of counselors. Perhaps, since the "ideal" is unattainable, we should capitalize on the many differences among the members of the school-counseling profession.

One additional note on the issue of counselor selection and preparation: As research continues in the area of counseling, it becomes more apparent that a "helper must be functioning at higher levels than the helpee in the relevant areas of concern" (Carkhuff 1969, p. xii). Helpers are at least assumed to be living more effectively than those they intend to help. If this assumption is accepted, school-counselors who are most likely to be successful are functioning at high levels personally and intellectually. The school-counseling profession does not need the person who obtains more benefits from counseling than the client. Among the many peer self-help groups, those who are rehabilitated help those in need; however the blind do not lead the blind. The ex-alcoholic, or ex-drug addict, can help people break their habits, but the person who is presently on drugs seldom helps anyone to break the habit. In fact, it might be argued that a person who is functioning at a low level unwittingly works to support the failure of others. The trend in the selection of future school-counselors will, no doubt, be toward identifying persons with high levels of personal functioning, intellectual ability, and interpersonal skill.

A fourth issue in school counseling is whether counselors should be taught a particular counseling theory or a variety of theories from which they may select the one most appropriate for themselves. The advocates of teaching only one approach to the prospective school-counselor feel that a counseling student would do well to learn one approach thoroughly in a master's degree program. Lack of time for learning additional approaches is one argument supporting their reasoning. That it is better to do one thing proficiently than a number ineffectively is another argument frequently presented. A counselor who learns one theory well also seems to develop a certain depth and consistency about his counseling. If a school-counselor clearly identifies with a particular theory, he can point to the research evidence supporting that theory as a justification for his effectiveness. Of course, if only one theory or approach is to be taught to prospective school-counselors, the next question is: Which one? Those who argue for teaching a number of approaches do not have to answer this question. Instead, they suggest that the counseling student be exposed to various theories and then select the one most suited to his personality and background. According to this argument, a person who is adroit, persuasive, and forceful can become an effective counselor by utilizing one of the more directive counseling theories, such as Albert Ellis's rational-emotive approach. Likewise, a more passive personality would adopt one of the theories that relies more on reflective techniques. Naturally the program teaching many approaches would need to focus considerable effort on helping the counseling student to determine his values, personality, and life-style in order to select a counseling theory consistent with these character traits.

There is really a third position on the issue of teaching one or more counseling theories—that is, to train eclectic counselors. Eclectic counselors do not adhere to any one theory but are taught to borrow techniques from many different approaches. Some propose that a prospective school-counselor should not be taught a particular theory at all, but should be helped to build his own counseling approach. However, making every school-counselor a theorist, while an ambitious idea, is unlikely to be accomplished.

The trend in counselor-education seems to be toward developing eclectic school-counselors. Because the school-counselor does not work with only one particular type of student problem, the eclectic approach seems sensible. Either contemporary school-counselors must receive general training, to enable them to reach a variety of students, or they must restrict their functions and become specialists who only counsel students with certain kinds of problems. Regardless of direction, generalist or specialist, it does seem that the trend is for school-counselors to be better versed in not only what they do (the practical) but why they do it (the theoretical).

Another issue in the field is whether there should be different levels of counselors functioning in the school?

Team-work has become an important administrative concept in public education. Teaching, administrative, and pupil-personnel teams are utilized in a number of the larger school districts. In most instances, the implication for the school-counselor is that he will either become a member of a team or learn to assist teams rather than individuals.

Another outgrowth of the idea of developing teams to accomplish educational tasks is the proposal that the school-counselor's functions be divided among various professional and paraprofessional personnel. Some school systems are developing guidance and counseling programs that employ support-personnel for the counselor. Paraprofessional counselors and counselor-aides are utilized in guidance and counseling functions in much the same way that teaching teams utilize teacher-aides. Those supporting the use of guidance-aides argue that counselors are presently engaging in too many routine or clerical functions, which might be done by members of lower career-levels. The development of such career-levels within the profession is also supported as a means of improving selection and recruitment procedures. For example, guidance-aide work might replace teaching as the entry position for school counseling. Those who oppose the levels concept in school-counseling argue that the services provided students should not be segmented. They point out that most educational programs are too fragmented now; that counselors have been unique in providing personal attention to the total student and his needs. There is also much concern that paraprofessionals and aides would be unable to handle real and personal information about students in a confidential manner. Regardless of the arguments against levels of counselor function and training, it would appear that more experimentation will be tried in the near future with aides and paraprofessionals.

Is the school-counselor primarily a counselor, or are there non-counseling functions as important as counseling, or even more important? While this question has some overlap with other questions, it does merit special discussion. There are those in the field of school counseling who feel the counselor's function should be limited to one-to-one or small-group counseling. Others propose that the school-counselor should teach classes in psychological education, direct in-service education programs for teachers, or assist teachers in developing behavioral-modification plans for their classrooms. The issue is more than whether the counselor should have playground or bus duties along with classroom teachers; rather, it centers around whether the counselor should stop counseling children and do other functions considered more productive. The critical question is whether the counselor would be more effective in helping children if he consulted with adults who have direct contact with students. Some say the counselor would do better to stop counseling students directly and teach them mental-health or psychological-education courses instead. A different point of view relates to working with them directly. At times, a counselor's attempt to manipulate environment results in conflict with administration, staff, or parents, all of whom may be attempting to manipulate conditions in a different direction. The debate will no doubt rage on for some time concerning whether the counselor should teach, consult, manipulate the environment, or counsel. Elementary-school counseling and guidance seems to be the area most sharply divided by this debate. Obviously, to resolve the debate is beyond the scope of this book. Two excellent sources of further discussion on this issue are Faust (1968) and Wrenn (1973, chap. 12).

One final issue to be discussed is whether school-counselors can effectively serve both their counselees and the institution and still survive as a profession. The school-counselor, like nearly every other social scientist and professional in our time, is faced with the conflict of determining whether to serve the individual or the social order. The choice is not an easy one—the counselor is hired by a social institution purportedly to help students identify and fulfill their individual needs, but at the same time he is expected to be "loyal" to the school.

Baker and Hansen (1972) have developed an inventory which assesses counselor style. An explanation of some of the alternatives available to school-counselors may convey some of the confusion about whether the counselor can serve the student and the institution simultaneously. Suppose a group of students approach the counselor about the homework and other "busy" work they have in one of their classes. There are many courses of action open to anyone receiving such a complaint. One alternative is to *counsel* the students to take some effective action about their concern. A counselor who does this functions as a counselor only. His position would be that his job, as school-counselor, is to help counselees determine what actions they should take. As a result of such counseling, the counselees take action, the counselors do not. In some circumstances, school-counselors have reacted to such complaints in other ways, and sometimes they have even taken action personally. The counselor might make a referral to the school principal based upon the assumption that the principal should handle problems about teachers. While counseling might ordinarily be thought to be a means of supporting the status quo, and referring a means of effecting change, this is not necessarily so. For example, by counseling the students in the case described above, the counselor might be supporting change, especially if he helps the students to find a way of moving from powerlessness to a base of power. On the other hand, by referring the students to the principal the counselor might be taking action to support the status quo, especially if he knows the principal will support the teacher regardless of circumstances.

Another alternative might be to get the students and the teacher together and help the two parties *negotiate* an effective solution to the problem. Oftentimes during such negotiations counselors are forced into the position of supporting one side or the other, thereby becoming arbiters who make a decision for others.

In still other instances the counselor might attempt to talk the students out of acting upon their concern. While this may not generally be considered commendable, there have been instances when school-counselors have supported the status quo by acting in such a manner. In a way, the counselor is acting as he thinks the administration would act, so in effect he is performing as an assistant administrator. In fairness to the counselor, conditions may have been such that he honestly feels he is justified in being judgmental (for example, the school may be in a state of near-riot because of poor student-teacher relations). Nonetheless, by doing so the counselor firmly aligns himself with the institution rather than with the students.

The counselor, rather than supporting the administration of the school or counseling the students, may take some action in the students' favor. Some counselor-educators and school-counselors urge that counselors should function as child-advocates by arguing the students' case for them. Such action is justified, according to this position, because the children are at a disadvantage and deserve an adult to argue their case against another adult. There is at least one other action open to the school-counselor. In some instances he might become a social advocate. He may actually support, organize, or lead the students to demonstrate against unfair conditions at the school. In other instances the counselor might organize power blocs other than the students; nonetheless he uses political action for social change. Of course there are some counselors who promote the idea of social activism but suggest approaches more subtle than walk-outs or demonstrations. Such suggestions are along the lines of the counselor identifying the power structure within the school and community, and working to manipulate the power-holders to modify the present system to better meet the needs of students. Numerous counselor-educators see counselors as being change-agents or advocates for change. The May 1971 issue of the *Personnel and Guidance Journal* was entirely devoted to the question of counselors and the social revolution.

There are those who feel that counselors must maintain a counseling function as exclusively as possible. Becoming involved in a "cause" interferes with the process of caring for the individual. As Halmos (1966, p. 25) says, "One can't care for persons and impersonal causes at the same time . . . " To be concerned with a cause and to make a difference in the cause one must be impersonal and hard.

Martin and Harrison (1972) are among those who feel that counselors would be better able to function both as counselors and as advocates if autonomous guidance and evaluation centers were set up in the community apart from the school. Perhaps, if such were the case, counselors could function directly to help students "make it" through school without having to worry about a direct conflict with the school, which might jeopardize their jobs. One of the future trends in this area may be the autonomous guidance center. Even without the autonomous center, it appears that school-counselors will continue to function as counselors, will function more as student advocates, and will function less as assistants to administrators. There are other possible trends in the field of school counseling. Key phrases for the future might very well be accountability for performance, collaboration with administrators, identification of power structures, and computer counseling. Determining the issues in school counseling is relatively easy because the conflicts are obvious. Listing and describing trends is much more difficult because there are so many factors and unknown influences. The only real certainty is that the future of school counseling is uncertain.

## RESEARCH ON THE EFFECTIVENESS OF
## SCHOOL COUNSELING

Any treatment of school counseling would be quite incomplete without some consideration of whether or not counseling makes a difference to students and other persons served by the counselor in the school and the community. In order to determine the degree of impact school-counselors have, two questions must be answered: (1) Does individual and group counseling effect positive results among counseled students? (2) Is the school-counselor considered helpful by those he serves?

Some research findings indicate that counseling does affect counselees in positive ways; however, conflicting research indicates that counseling is ineffective. Moreover, in some cases, the findings indicate that counseling has detrimental effects on those counseled. Because of the conflicting evidence, there is considerable debate about the efficacy of counseling. The many critics seem to overlook the number of studies showing the benefits of both individual and group counseling.

One classic study on the effects of counseling was reported by Campbell (1965). The study was a twenty-five-year follow-up comparing college students who were counseled with a matched group who had not been counseled. The evidence showed that the impact of counseling on student "achievements" decreased over time; however, there were still significant differences for counseled males as compared to noncounseled males. Campbell therefore concluded that counseling did exert beneficial effects.

Rothney's studies (1958) of secondary school counseling in Wisconsin showed results favoring the counseled students after a five-year follow-up. A ten-year follow-up led to the generalization that counseled students were much more likely to complete some form of post-high school training than were the noncounseled students.

Two studies show the more immediate effects of counseling in the schools. One study by Schmieding (1966) indicated that counseling and guidance procedures applied by well-trained school-counselors had two effects upon failing junior high school students. The counseled students had higher levels of academic achievement and better teacher-student relationships. Another study, this one conducted by Kinnick and Shannon (1965), showed that peer-group acceptance can be improved by the use of individual and group approaches in the school.

Some of the studies investigating the counseling of elementary school students show conflicting results. Anderson (1968) concluded, after studying 327 elementary school children in grades four, five, and six, that individual counseling was effective, especially in promoting self-concept growth. Kennedy and Thompson (1967), using behavioral-counseling techniques with first-grade students, showed positive results concerning behavior and work completion. In contrast, Alper and Kranzler (1970), in a study comparing client-centered and behavioral approaches, found the effects on students counseled to be insignificant. They concluded that "talking" to children in a counselor's office is usually a waste of time. A critique of their research strongly refuted some of this study's conclusions and suggested that additional research should be conducted (Burck, Cottingham, and Reardon 1973, p. 225).

Positive results are shown by some of the research on counseling primarily aimed at effecting specific behavioral changes for counselees. Welch (1971) conducted a study with sixteen overweight adolescent girls and concluded that "talking" with these students about their approach to weight loss, combined with weight measurement, produced significant weight losses in six weeks. A reality-therapy counseling approach was used to obtain the weight losses. Measurements of self-concept change did not prove to be significant; therefore, Welch concluded that effective counseling changes behaviors before it changes attitudes. Benson and Blocher (1967), in a study very similar to Welch's, also predicted specific behavioral changes, and were able to show positive results by using a developmental small-group approach with low-achieving high school students.

Some additional conclusions about school counseling are available from Leona Tyler (1969), who has been reviewing counseling research since 1953:

1. Counseling does help students achieve somewhat more success both while they are in school and after they graduate.
2. The "ideal" and "real" self-concepts of counselees become more alike after both brief educational-vocational counseling and more extensive personal counseling.
3. Students with academic potential are helped to improve achievement by short-term counseling focused on identifying corrective behaviors.
4. Vocational counseling improves vocational adjustment.
5. There is little evidence to show a difference in effectiveness between individual and group counseling.

6. The personal qualities of school-counselors differentiate effective from ineffective counselors better than differences in theoretical point of view on counseling.
7. Guidance programs in schools have positive impact on students.

Tyler's work merits considerable study by school-counselors and others interested in evaluating the impact of the school-counselor. Another of Tyler's conclusions, not listed above, is somewhat in contradiction with Armour's study reported below. Tyler found that counseled students, by a four-to-one margin, consistently reported the counseling experience as more helpful than not helpful. Armour (1969) found less positive perceptions about the counselor's service when all students, both counseled and noncounseled, were surveyed.

These findings relate to a final area of concern: whether students view the counselor as helpful. Is the school-counselor considered helpful by those he serves? One extensive report answers this question with an emphatic no. The survey research of Armour, completed in 1969, indicated that counselors were considered a less important source of advice than members of the family. In some communities, school-counselors were also rated lower than teachers and friends as a source of help. It is interesting to note that counselors were regarded more favorably in urban working-class and semirural mixed communities than in suburban middle-class areas.

Armour's study also reported how often students were counseled during the course of a year. Fourteen percent never saw the counselor and only 10 percent saw the counselor six or more times. Fifty-six percent of the students saw their counselor two to five times during the school-year. It is hard to imagine the school-counselor having a significant impact on students seen only once or twice.

Armour's study investigated the effect of counseling on student aspirations and self-concepts. The results favored the counseled students, but did not show significant differences between counseled and uncounseled students. The research design had serious limitations; however, two significant findings noted that counselors tend to see those students needing less help, and that counselors seem to have more impact on lower-socioeconomic-class students.

Boy and Pine (1968) reported an evaluation of a counseling program in a junior high school. Among the findings were: (1) seventy-two percent of the students had voluntary contact with the school-counselor during the second year of the program; (2) eighty-four percent of the students who used the counseling service rated it as worthwhile, very helpful, or extremely helpful, while sixteen percent rated it as of little help, of no help, or did not respond; (3) over half of the students reported help in becoming better learners, learning about "myself," and making "life's work" decisions.

Erpenbach (1973), writing about testimony before Congress in support of guidance and counseling in the schools, quotes from a Gallup Poll finding that 83 percent of high school juniors and seniors felt guidance counselors were "worth the added cost." Parents with children in school answered the same question positively 79 percent of the time. Even among parents without children in school, 69 percent were in favor of paying the cost of school-counselors. Erpenbach concludes that schools need more counselors before the effectiveness of counseling can be adequately demonstrated.

Not all the research on school counseling has been reviewed here. A helpful volume for those interested in more intensive study is the recent work of Burck, Cottingham, and Reardon (1973). Perhaps the best conclusion to be drawn at this time is that individual and group counseling in the schools may be for better, for worse, or for no effect at all.

In summary it appears, from a brief review of the evidence, that counseling does in fact make a difference frequently enough to merit considerable attention and research in the future. With careful attention to proficient practice and continued endeavors to conduct pertinent research, school counseling may yet become a positive force for improving schools and enriching the lives of individual students.

## REFERENCES

Alper, T., and Kranzler, G. 1970. "A Comparison of the Effectiveness of Behavioral and Client-centered Approaches for the Behavior Problems of Elementary School Children." *Elementary School Guidance and Counseling* 5:35-43.

Anderson, E. C. 1968. "Counseling and Consultation versus Teacher-consultation in the Elementary School." *Elementary School Guidance and Counseling* 2:276-85.

Armour, D. 1969. *The American School Counselor*. New York: Russell Sage Foundation.

Baker, S., and Hansen, J. 1972. "School Counselor Attitudes on a Status Quo-Change Agent Measurement Scale." *School Counselor* 19:243-48.

Benson, R., and Blocher, D. 1967. "Evaluation of Developmental Counseling with Groups of Low Achievers in a High School Setting." *School*

*Counselor* 14:215-20.

Boy, A., and Pine, G. 1968. *The Counselor in the Schools: A Reconceptualization.* New York: Houghton-Mifflin.

Burck, H.; Cottingham, H.; and Reardon, R. 1973. *Counseling and Accountability: Methods and Critique.* New York: Pergamon Press.

Campbell, D. 1965. "Achievements of Counseled and Non-counseled Students Twenty-five Years After Counseling." *Journal of Counseling Psychology* 12:287-93.

Carkhuff, R. 1969. *Helping and Human Relations.* New York: Holt, Rinehart, & Winston.

Cowen, E. 1971. "Emergent Directions in School Mental Health." *American Scientist* 59:723-32.

Erpenbach, W. 1973. "The Case for Guidance: Testimony before Congress." *Personnel and Guidance Journal* 51:551-57.

Faust, V. *Establishing Guidance Programs in Elementary Schools.* New York: Houghton-Mifflin.

Halmos, P. 1966. *The Faith of the Counselors.* New York: Schocken Books.

Kennedy, D., and Thompson, I. 1967. "Use of Reinforcement Techniques with a First Grade Boy." *Personnel and Guidance Journal* 46:366-70.

Kinnick, B., and Shannon, J. 1965. "The Effect of Counseling on Peer Group Acceptance of Socially Rejected Students." *School Counselor* 12:162-66.

Martin, J., and Harrison, C. 1972. *Free to Learn, Unlocking and Ungrading American Education.* Englewood Cliffs, N.J.: Prentice-Hall.

Nelson, R. 1972. *Guidance and Counseling.* New York: Holt, Rinehart & Winston.

Peters, H. 1970. "The Counselor as a Developer." In *Counseling and Guidance in the Twentieth Century,* ed. W. Van Hoose and J. Pietrofesa. New York: Houghton-Mifflin.

Rothney, J. 1958. *Guidance Practices and Results.* New York: Harper & Brothers.

Schmieding, O. 1966. "An Investigation of Efficacy of Counseling and Guidance Procedures with Failing Junior High Students." *School Counselor* 14:14, 74-80.

Tyler, L. 1969. *The Work of the Counselor.* New York: Appleton-Century-Crofts.

Welch, R. 1971. "A Weight Loss Program for Overweight Adolescent Girls and Its Effects on Self-Concepts." Unpublished dissertation, University of Tennessee, Knoxville.

Wrenn, C. 1973. *The World of the Contemporary Counselor.* Boston: Houghton-Mifflin.

# Bibliography

ARBUCKLE, D. *Counseling: Philosophy, Theory, and Practice.* 2d ed. Boston: Allyn & Bacon, 1970. One of the most nearly complete counseling books available. Discusses philosophy of counseling, counselor, nature of counseling, and counseling experience. Perhaps strongest part of book is very good way it handles issues in profession. All sides of question are presented and well-referenced.

BENJAMIN, A. *The Helping Interview.* Boston: Houghton-Mifflin, 1969. One of the better books on how to do counseling. Considers following counseling topics: conditions, stages, philosophy, recording interviews, and using questions, communications, responses, and leads. Many questions answered for beginning counselor who wants to know what to do when.

BOROW, H. *Career Guidance for a New Age.* Atlanta: Houghton-Mifflin, 1973. Important articles on history of vocational guidance, social change, and nature of work. Two chapters present practical suggestions for vocational counseling and guidance activities in schools.

BURCK, H.; COTTINGHAM, H.; and REARDON, R. *Counseling and Accountability: Methods and Critique.* New York: Pergamon Press, 1973. Nine chapters on conceptual foundations of theory and research in counseling. Addressed to wide audience from social workers to vocational-rehabilitation workers; eight of the studies were conducted in school settings. Authors do more than tell how to criticize research, they actually do extremely concise, direct critiques. Book would be helpful to students who need to critique research or write research proposal.

HANSEN, J.; STEVIE, R.; and WARNER, R. *Counseling: Theory and Process.* Boston: Allyn & Bacon, 1972. Recommended for school-counselor in training. Presents chapter on counseling theory, practice, and research followed by chapters on contributions to counseling from psychoanalytic theory, self-theory, and learning theory. Roles of diagnosis, relationship, decision-making, and testing also treated. Chapter on vocational counseling helpful for those interested in career education. Concluding chapter on ethics, legalities, and values in counseling. Annotated bibliographies at end of each chapter quite helpful for those who wish to search further. In fact, our readers should peruse original sources cited in this text for first-hand knowledge of each theoretical approach presented.

NELSON, R. *Guidance and Counseling in the Elementary School.* New York: Holt, Rinehart, & Winston, 1972. Very comprehensive textbook for those who want understanding of functions of elementary-school counselor. Four chapters focus on group and individual counseling with schoolchildren. Takes position that there is no single right way to counsel since several different approaches offer helpful methods. Need for guidance and counseling in elementary school well documented. Review of research and suggestions for research still needed on effectiveness of counseling in schools.

PATTERSON, C. *Theories of Counseling and Psychotherapy.* New York: Harper & Row, 1966. Excellent summary of several major approaches to counseling. Covers rational, learning-theory, psychoanalytic, perceptual-phenomenological, and existential viewpoints. Concluding chapter examines divergences and convergences in counseling. Provides thorough introduction to some classical approaches to counseling. Also included, some sample counseling interviews followed by summary and evaluation of each theory.

PETERS, H. *The Guidance Process: A Perspective.* Itasca, Ill.: F. E. Peacock, 1970. Presents this guidance leader's ideas about "guidance process." Not intended to present specific principles, techniques, tools, or programs; nonetheless challenges practicing school-counselors to reconsider many of their daily functions and responsibilities.

THOMPSON, C., and POPPEN, W. *For Those Who Care: Ways of Relating to Youth.* Columbus: Charles E. Merrill, 1972. Practical book of interest to school-counselors, teachers, and parents. Presents counseling approach to "relating to youth." Details specific techniques for managing conflicts, and for developing learning partnerships, group activities, and behavior change, as aid for counselors, educators, and parents seeking to put theory into practice.

TYLER, L. *The Work of the Counselor.* New York: Appleton-Century-Crofts, 1969. Popularity of this book is demonstrated by fact that it is presently in third edition. Author believes every counselor should develop unique counseling approach. Outlines process for forming one's own point of view. Especially helpful are research summaries. Although stresses theory-building and research, also treats practical topics, such as how to start initial counseling interview.

VAN HOOSE, W.; and PIETROFESA, J., eds. *Counseling and Guidance in the Twentieth Century: Reflections and Reformulations.* New York: Houghton-Mifflin, 1970. Original contributions from the following leaders in counseling and guidance: D. Arbuckle, H. Borow, G. Farwell, E. Ginzberg, G. Hill, R. Hoppock, K. Hoyt, E. Lloyd-Jones, R. Mathewson, C. Miller, M. Ohlsen, C. Patterson, H. Peters, E. Roeber, J. Rothney, J. Samler, B. Stefflre, R. Strang, A. Traxler, L. Tyler, E. Williamson, and C. Wrenn.

WRENN, C. *The World of the Contemporary Counselor*. Boston: Houghton-Mifflin, 1973. Not a book about counseling, except for last two chapters, "Counseling and Caring, 1 & 2." Rather, treats world of counselors as persons and worlds of counselors' students. Wrenn, with help of research assistant Lynn Leonard, helps "encapsulated counselor" more completely to understand contemporary youth.